THE ORDER OF THE ROSE

THE LIFE AND IDEAS OF CHRISTINE DE PIZAN

Christine de Pizan. Harleian MS 4431. A similar picture, showing her almost invariably in the same blue gown, appears in large numbers of her manuscripts.

Photo British Library.

The Order of the Rose

THE LIFE AND IDEAS OF
CHRISTINE DE PIZAN

By

ENID McLEOD

ROWMAN AND LITTLEFIELD
TOTOWA, NEW JERSEY

First published in the United States 1976
by ROWMAN AND LITTLEFIELD, Totowa, N.J.

ISBN 0 87471 810 4

Printed in Great Britain

To bring the dead to life
Is no great magic.
Few are wholly dead:
Blow on a dead man's embers
And a live flame will start.

ROBERT GRAVES

Contents

Illustrations

Note to the Reader

Every circumstance in the life of Christine mentioned in the following text, every expression of her thoughts and feelings, and every actual quotation of her words, is taken from her own books, principally from two of them, *La Mutacion de Fortune* and *Lavision*, but also from autobiographical statements scattered about in other writings of hers. To have given page references to the critical editions of these (which incidentally are not easy to come by outside state and specialist libraries), as I first thought of doing, would have meant that the pages, especially of the first three chapters, were peppered with numbers, almost one to every sentence. I therefore abandoned this practice, except in the case of one or two statements of particular importance, and one or two quotations, whose source is given. Again, apart from one or two cases where the French is relatively simple, all the quotations are translated, as Christine's fifteenth-century French would present great difficulties for the general reader.

Foreword

For anyone unable, as I am, to read fifteenth-century French manuscripts, it would not have been possible to write this book forty years ago. For with the exception of four of Christine's books which were printed during the hundred years after her death her works remained in manuscript for over three centuries. And although she herself was widely known during her lifetime and remembered by her fellow writers in France in the sixteenth century, even her name was thereafter forgotten in France, the country she had served so well.

An effort to revive a knowledge of her and her writings was made in the eighteenth century by Mademoiselle de Keralio, who in 1787 brought out her *Collection des meilleurs ouvrages françois composés par des femmes*. The second volume of this contained an excellent short account of Christine's life by M. Boivin le jeune, and notes on two of Christine's manuscripts by the Abbé Sallier. And in that and the third volume there are descriptions, some short and some quite long, of a good many of Christine's works and considerable extracts or abridged versions of others. Mlle de Keralio herself contributed a short appreciation of Christine's character and abilities.

But this attempt to revive the memory of Christine and her writings failed to arouse the slightest interest in them among the scholars of the time. And when in the mid-nineteenth and twentieth centuries they became at last a subject of serious study, Mlle de Keralio herself suffered a similar neglect for hardly any recent scholars mention her.

The first to rescue Christine from this obscurity was Raymond Thomassy, who in his *Essai sur les écrits politiques de Christine de Pisan*, published in 1838, not only wrote most perceptively, particularly on those writings of Christine's concerned with contemporary France, but printed two of the shorter but most significant of them. Even after this, forty years passed before other aspects of her work were studied. The first general book on her, E. M.-D. Robineau's *Christine de Pisan, sa vie, ses oeuvres*, appeared in 1882, followed four years later by Maurice Roy's fine three-volume edition of her poetic works. Thereafter there have been a number of general works in France, and in the last forty years of this century many scholars, chiefly women, both in France and America have been bringing out critical editions of her various books. Some however still await attention.

But in England scant attention has been paid to her, either by scholars or general writers. There have been some translations of her poems, and in 1913 Alice Kemp-Welch wrote a good but brief summary of her life in a book called *Of Six Mediaeval Women*. This it was which first implanted her name in my mind, many years ago. But there has been no full-scale account of Christine and her works. It is therefore hoped that the present book may fill that gap and do something to restore this remarkable woman to the esteem in which the English held her five centuries ago.

ENID McLEOD

CHAPTER ONE

The Astrologer's Daughter

ONE of the more civilised aspects of life in Europe, before the chauvinism of the last hundred or two years largely put an end to the practice, was that gifted or eminent men were often invited to work in other countries than their own, apparently without causing any resentment among their fellow-specialists in those countries. This was particularly the case throughout the Middle Ages, when the sentiment of nationalism had not yet caged each race behind its own frontiers; and France in those days was a notable example of the custom. Thus it was apparently regarded as perfectly reasonable for Charlemagne, in the eighth century, to invite the Englishman Alcuin to his court, with the mission of reviving learning in his kingdom and creating schools where Latin grammar in particular was to be taught. Four centuries later another learned English Latinist, John of Salisbury, having taught in the schools of Chartres, was made bishop there.

So it was in accordance with tradition when Charles V of France, on acceding to the throne in 1364 after eight years as dauphin and regent during the imprisonment of his father in England, invited an Italian professor, Tommaso di Benvenuto da Pizzano, to come to his court as resident astrologer and physician. Tommaso, whose name derived from the village of Pizzano in the foothills near Bologna where he had been born, had studied medicine and astrology at the University of Bologna to such purpose that in 1342 he was elected by the medical students to a lectureship, or it may be a chair, of astrology there. In 1357 an older friend of his, Tommaso di Mondini da Forli, who was a salaried councillor of the Republic of Venice, obtained a similar post for the younger Tommaso, who held it for seven years, and lived there in considerable state.

These meagre facts, which are all that the contemporary archives record of his early career in his own country,[1] do not suggest that he was in any way outstanding. But he must have been a man of considerable learning, since his fame had spread so far throughout Europe that not only Charles V of France but King Louis I of Hungary pressed him to come to their courts. These invitations, flattering though they were, did not tempt Tommaso greatly. He had begun to put down roots in his own country and was buying properties in other villages round Bologna—a small farm with a house and a vineyard for one, partly with the help of Tommaso di Mondini—and presumably had every intention of settling down there. He was in fact in Bologna on some business when the royal invitations reached him.

But there was another reason why he did not wish to leave his home. While he was in Venice he had married Mondini's daughter, and in 1363 -64, a year or so before the invitations came, he and his wife had had a daughter, whom they called Cristina. The invitation was for himself alone, and to leave his wife with such a very young child would be a big step to take. On the other hand he had a great longing to see the court of the most famous king in Europe; and equally, for the man of learning that he was, it was a wonderful chance to see something of the great University of Paris. So in the end he decided to go, intending to stay for one year only. Before he went he transported his little family to their home near Bologna. And in the year 1364 he left for Paris.

There he found himself one of a company of brilliant men, for Charles V, himself an intellectual with a well-furnished and subtle mind, had a passion for learning and loved to surround himself with 'solemn clerks, philosophers grounded in mathematical and speculative sciences'.[2] He at once took to Thomas de Pizan as the French, with their well-known habit of gallicising foreign names wherever possible, called him, and held him in great affection from then until the end of his days. Although the king sometimes referred to him as 'our astronomer and beloved and loyal physician'[3] it was as an astrologer that he chiefly prized him; for Charles had great faith in this pseudo-science, which some of his more advanced advisers were beginning to despise.

So much did the king come to rely on his astrologer that, when the year was up, he tried to persuade him to stay on, by offering to pay the cost of bringing his family to Paris, and to give Thomas such emoluments as would let them live there in very comfortable circumstances. Thomas still wanted to go back to his native land, but to please the king he stayed on from year to year until three more had passed, after which he gave in and sent for his wife and the little Cristina, who was by now four to five years old. The upheaval of leaving home must have been great for the mother, and the journey long and tiring in one of those litters that were no better than a wooden box on wooden wheels. But for the child it was obviously an exciting adventure, for later she remembered vividly how they passed through 'strange countries, over high alps and across wild plains, through deep forests and rushing rivers'. No wonder it made a deep impression, for it was the only time in her life that she was ever to travel. And she was never again to see the land of her birth.

They reached Paris in the autumn of 1368 and that December they were presented to the king and his court. The ceremony must have been a formal and general one of some importance, for it took place at the Louvre, a palace the king used only for state occasions. For it the child and her mother wore richly adorned clothes after the Lombard fashion, suitable, Christine said later, for women of state; and so they were thus able to vie with what must have been a splendidly dressed throng. For the king, though by nature and in his private life austere in his ways and tastes, held strongly that on public occasions a great monarch should appear as magnificently as possible. It pleased him too that his queen, Jane of Bourbon, to whom he was tenderly devoted, should be sumptuously arrayed in splendid robes and should glitter with the jewels he delighted to give her. The princes of the blood and the other nobles and courtiers were not loath to follow the king's example as far as they could, so that the scene must have been a dazzling one for the child and her mother.

But however regally crowned and resplendently robed the king may have been, there was nothing in his physique to intimidate a child. He was still a young man, only thirty-two, and his face was that of a gentle scholar rather than a man of action. He had a high forehead, a thin spiky nose, and pale sunken cheeks with high cheekbones which made him look what he was, a man who in his early youth had had grave illnesses and who suffered still, with fevers and neuralgia. His frame was thin too, and he had a badly swollen right hand, which meant that he could never wield a sword. With all this his general expression, as one can see from the few representations of him that exist, was one of great benevolence and understanding. He could not of course have talked to the little Italian girl, as she did not yet understand French. But it may well be that, as he looked down at her, the seeds of that fervent admiration of him that she felt all her life were sown in her at that time. For Christine de Pizan,[4] as she was thenceforward called, was to become one of his most loyal subjects and a great patriot of her adopted country.

On this occasion, she says, he was surrounded by a splendid company of his relations. These could have been none other than his three brothers, the Dukes of Anjou, Berry and Burgundy, the princes of the *fleur-de-lis* as they were called. Anjou was always known as the King of Sicily because he was the adopted son of Queen Jane of Naples and Sicily, and this far-away kingdom so dominated his thoughts that he took comparatively little part in French affairs. John, Duke of Berry, was unlike his royal brother in appearance, being plump and self-indulgent looking, but like him a great lover of jewels and works of art in general, and the chief object of his life was the acquiring and com-missioning of them to adorn the palaces in his apanage of Berry and the Limousin, at the expense of his reluctant subjects. Philip, the third brother, had gained his nickname of 'the Bold' when at the age of only fourteen he had fought beside his father at the battle of Poitiers, in 1356. His great apanage of the dukedom and county of Burgundy which Charles V had given him on returning from his coronation in 1364, made him a richer and more powerful figure than the king himself; but Burgundy was a great admirer of his brother and always loyal to him. Both Berry and Burgundy were to become considerable benefactors to Christine; but it is hardly likely that so young a child could have been aware of them on this occasion.

The Paris in which Charles V had invited Thomas de Pizan and his family to come and live was a peaceful and prosperous city, very different from what it had been only ten years earlier. Discontent and misery had begun to be rife there under his father King John. But when he was taken captive to England after the defeat of the French at Poitiers, the government of his officers and the remaining nobles became so corrupt, and the condition of the citizens so wretched, that open revolt broke out. This was led by Etienne Marcel, the Provost of the merchants of Paris, who claimed that he spoke for all the citizens, but who represented chiefly the burgesses, who wanted more power for themselves. To add to the dangers of the uprising, the King of Navarre, a friend of Etienne Marcel, joined forces with him, thinking that this would be a good moment to challenge the authority of the reigning house of Valois. Feeling soon ran so high that in 1358 they burst into the royal palace on the *Ile de la Cité* and before the eyes of the dauphin Charles murdered some of his councillors, spattering his robes with their blood.

Charles who, when all this began, had been a sickly adolescent, had in that year just been named regent. With this accession of power he at once began to show his mettle, for he had the courage to go alone and address a gathering of the burgesses in one of their strongholds, the Halles; and there is almost an Elizabethan ring about a speech he made his 'good people', as he was always to call them, in which he told them he had come to live and die among them. He was not of course able to restore peace immediately, and for some time there were still occasional outbreaks of violence, in one of which Etienne Marcel himself was killed. But gradually, by force of character, Charles quelled Navarre and was able to dominate all unruly elements; and because of his own innate qualities and understanding of the needs of his subjects, he was able to restore good government and the prestige that still clung to the person of royalty, while himself always remaining approachable by his people. So when in 1364 he finally became king, his capital was once again a peaceful place.

It was a beautiful and well-planned city as well as a peaceful one. Guillebert de Metz, who in old age wrote his *Description de la Ville de Paris au XVe siècle*,[5] described the city as he remembered it when he first came there as a student in the time of Charles V. It was, he says, divided into three separate sections. In what he calls the High Town, on the left bank of the Seine, was the university, lying on the rising ground of the Montagne Sainte Geneviève. The principal inhabitants there were the students, in lodgings all round the university. The king had given a new importance to the university because of the deep interest he took in learning himself, principally in philosophy and Latin, and his habit of inviting the professors of it, under their famous chancellor, Jean Gerson, to come and talk with him. There were one or two great abbeys in that quarter too, like those of Saint Victor and Saint Germain-des-Prés, whose tower still dominates this part of the city. And there was too at least one great ducal house, that of the Duke of Berry, called the Hôtel de Nesles, whose Tour de Nesles remained a landmark by the river for centuries to come.

The second section of Paris, known then, as it still is, as the *Cité*, was in part the seat of ecclesiastical affairs because of the Cathedral of Notre Dame with the houses of its canons clustering round it. But it was also the centre of government and administration; for the *Parlement* of Paris, the supreme court of justice, where the king sometimes sat in judgment, was housed in the huge hall of the old royal palace. The king's Council also met there, and the *Chambre des Comptes*, which controlled financial matters, was lodged there too. Guillebert de Metz adds a vivid reminiscent touch which enlivens the picture of these rather

17

solemn proceedings. He remembers, he says, that beside the palace there used to live a pewterer who kept some remarkable nightingales, which sang in winter. This palace had in fact been the principal dwelling of the kings of France in the past and there were still apartments in it for the royal family and the twelve peers of the realm. But Charles V, with his unhappy memories of the bloody scene that had taken place there in 1358, did not often stay there, preferring another palace which he himself had built in the third section of Paris, which Guillebert de Metz calls the Low Town, on the right bank of the river.

This was the Hôtel de Saint Pol,[6] which stood at the extreme eastern end of the sector covering all that part of modern Paris which lies between the Boulevard Saint Antoine and the river, with only the convent of the Celestines separating it from the open country. It was not a new building but a collection of great houses which the king had begun to buy in 1361 when he was still only regent. As he acquired more and more of these from their owners he welded them all into one, with long galleries and cloisters joining their gardens and great courtyards together, until in the end the whole complex was so vast that it comprised sets of apartments not only for the king and queen and their children but for all the princes of the blood, each with its own chapel, as well as all the necessary offices and rooms for their servants. Great sums and much imagination and taste were lavished on the decorations, as one can guess from such descriptions as that of the queen's chapel, which was painted in a bright shade of green known as *vert gai* in a design of flowers and fruit-trees— cherries, pears and plums—with children plucking fruit from the branches which soared up to the vaulted ceiling painted like a sky in blue and white. It was thus no wonder that the king, who as he said himself, had known many pleasures there, particularly that of recovering his health after some of the illnesses from which he so frequently suffered, held the palace so dear that he decreed in a moving document that it should remain an inalienable part of the domaine of the crown in perpetuity.*

This was by far the biggest building in this part of the Low Town, but there were other great houses too, notably the hôtel of the Duke of

---

* The fact that even a great king has no power to conserve a building after his own lifetime is sadly proved by the fact that, in spite of this decree, after the death of his son Charles VI, who also lived there, the palace was abandoned. His successors gave portions of it away and much of it fell into ruins, so that nothing of it now remains.

Anjou, the Hôtel d'Artois which belonged to the Duke of Burgundy, and one spectacular turreted building at the western end, which belonged to the king's brother-in-law, the Duke of Bourbon, another of the great dukes who was to become a particular friend of Christine de Pizan. There were great official buildings too, such as the Châtelet, the residence of one of the king's principal officers, the Provost of Paris, and the assembly hall of the powerful burgesses. And in the two hundred narrow streets in which these were set were the dwellings of the citizens of all classes. A notable feature of these streets was the great chains that in times of war were slung across them to protect the citizens from invaders.

But in the time of Charles V there was no longer any need for such protection, for the Low Town was not only a peaceful but a busy and prosperous place. With their king and so many of the princes living amongst them there was work not only for all the trades-people supplying the daily wants of the court and the great households but for all the artisans too, such was the king's passion for beautiful objects of all kinds. There were for instance the goldsmiths and silversmiths who fashioned all the utensils for the table and for daily household use, since only precious metals were used for these purposes. Some of these craftsmen in fact, says Guillebert de Metz, lived in the houses on the *Grand Pont* (now the *Pont au Change*) where the money-changers also lived. Some of the jewellers lived there too, and these the king kept largely employed for not only, as we know, did he love beautiful jewels for personal adornment, but he needed them also, set with great cabochon precious stones, for use as reliquaries, or to give as presents to important visitors. It must be remembered also that jewelry was a way of storing surplus wealth at a time when there were no banks, so that these rich objects could be melted down when money was needed for such necessary expenditure as the payment of soldiers, or for ransoms. Other craftsmen whom the king employed were the leather workers who made the sumptuous bindings for the fine manuscripts he had made for his library. The jewellers were needed for these too, to make the clasps of gold and silver which protected them. The king provided work for weavers of tapestries too, which hung on the walls of his many palaces, interspersed with the frescoes whose painters also were treated rather as superior artisans than as artists, and were spoken of as the king's valets.

Charles V provided much work for the stone-masons too, together with the stone-carvers and wood-workers, for in addition to the Hôtel de

Saint Pol he was busy building other royal palaces in the surroundings of Paris, the great castle of Vincennes for one, another at Saint-Germain-en-Laye, and the delightfully named Beauté on the Marne. In Paris itself at that time he also rebuilt the Louvre, getting his master-mason, Raymond du Temple, to transform it outwardly from the old fortress which Philip Augustus had put up two centuries earlier, into the fairy-tale castle that we see in the *Très Riches Heures du Duc de Berry*, with its clusters of conical-roofed towers separated from the river only by a low crenellated wall and a broad green terrace. But in spite of its charming new outward appearance, Charles still kept it mainly as a fortress and an arsenal to protect the town at the extreme western end, using its great halls only for such occasions as that at which Christine had been presented to him. And to balance it as a protection for the town at the eastern end, he built the fortress of the Bastille.

But the king was not only concerned to build public palaces and others for his own habitation. Immediately to the west of the Hôtel de Saint Pol—and indeed their gardens touched—stood the large Hôtel de Sens, which belonged to the Archbishop of Sens. In 1365 the king bought it from the archbishop, lodging him elsewhere, and had it joined on to his own property in order, as the *ordonnance* expressing his intention states, that he might construct within it 'many habitations as dwellings for the people of our household and our officers, so that they may better and more conveniently serve us and our successors. And we mean to acquire other manors adjoining our hôtel for the same purpose and that all should be more ample and spacious.'

Since this reconstruction must have been completed by the time Christine and her mother arrived in Paris, it seems not unlikely that one of the habitations comprised in it was the hostel that the king had promised to provide Thomas with for himself and his family. In addition to this free lodging, in 1372 the generous king gave Thomas the fief of Orsonville, in the commune of Villiers-en-Bière, to the south-east of Paris and east of Melun, which was worth an annual rent of twenty Parisian pounds.[7] Besides these properties and continual gifts of books and other presents, the king paid Thomas a regular salary of one hundred francs a month so that, soon after he received the fief of Orsonville, which from that reference to the worth of the rent it sounds as if he let, Thomas was well enough off to buy for his own occupation in the same neighbourhood a castle with the charming name of Mémorant.

But wherever Christine and her parents lived during her childhood she was happy, for she tells us she was a merry child, always laughing and singing. She had, she says, the knack of pleasing people, so that everyone vied to do things for her and to give her presents. And if anything upset her, her mother and her nurse were there to soothe and spoil her. She found it rather difficult at first to learn a language different from that of her parents, but her youthful senses and quick perceptions soon enabled her to adapt herself to the ways of her new country. All these things she tells us in the poems[8] she wrote later and in the brief passages referring to her early life scattered through other books. In two of these particularly, the *Mutacion de Fortune* and *Lavision* (which she always wrote in one word), there are whole pages that are most valuable, partly for the light they shed on the customs of the time, but chiefly because they paint a vivid picture of Christine and her parents in those early years in a way that is most rare in medieval writing, when it was not customary for a writer to mention such autobiographical material.

Her father, she relates, before her birth had greatly desired a son, who would be able to inherit his possessions, which presumably in ordinary families a girl might not do. His wife sympathised with his wish, but all the same really wanted a girl — 'a female like herself', as Christine was at pains to stress. But when the child was born, her mother also seems to have been disappointed at first, for her daughter was not at all like her, but resembled her father in looks and ways. No doubt she was able to console her husband for, although not learned — indeed she herself did not believe that women should be educated — she had a woman's wit and knew how to manage him. She was a cheerful person too, Christine says, and a very tender and loving mother, who so cherished her daughter that she had not a care in the world and at first only wanted to play with other children.

In later life Christine was to wish she had acquired the knowledge possessed by her father, for whose learning she developed a deep admiration that nothing was ever to lessen, even when some parts of it, particularly his astrology, began to seem to others out-of-date and even rather absurd. In childhood, however, this was denied her because she was a girl. One can almost sense the rage she felt later when she says of the refusal to educate girls that it was 'more by custom than right. If right prevailed, a daughter would gain as much as a son.' She was the more bitter about this in retrospect because, she says, 'I had a real desire for it and also great talent'. But it was useless to protest at the time, and one is inclined to doubt whether in fact she had this 'real desire' in childhood.

Indeed at one point, in looking back, she was fair-minded enough to admit that, as with most small children, it is their desire to play that keeps them from the schoolroom, unless they fear beating. As she had no such fear, the wish to play got the upper hand. So all she did was to pick up scraps of her father's knowledge, gleaned from being much in his company; but she says 'I had nothing unless I stole it'.*

Meanwhile there was the pleasure of growing up in that beautiful city where there was always something to see going on. Narrow and crowded though the streets may have been, there was a wide stretch of land beside the Seine, running all the way from the Louvre to the Hôtel de Saint Pol, for the houses were not built down to the water's edge. Here it was possible to walk and enjoy watching the traffic of the river passing up and down and going under the two bridges, the *Grand Pont* and the *Pont Notre Dame*. Another spectacle which must have exercised the kind of fascination that such things always do, on grown-ups and children alike, was the construction which the king had put in hand in 1367 of a new wall, enclosing all but the river side of the Low Town, complete with square towers and many gates, with a moat outside, part of which was to be used for public baths. This wall had become necessary because the rapidly growing town was bursting out of the old wall of Philip Augustus.

There were often more exciting scenes also. 'C'etait une grande chose que Paris', cries Guillebert de Metz nostalgically, 'quant on y voyait les rois de France, de Navarre et de Sicile, quand plusieurs ducs, comtes, prelates et autres notables seigneurs y demeuraient ordinairement'. And he recalls how what he calls the Emperors of Greece and Rome and other kings used to come there to enjoy themselves. The arrival of these visitors meant that there were grand processions to watch, but none thrilled Christine more than those of Charles V, when he rode through the narrow streets, as he frequently did, on his way to one or other of his many palaces in the surroundings of Paris.

These cavalcades were a glittering spectacle which she never forgot;[9] for the king would not suffer his young knights and esquires to be less than richly apparelled and splendidly mounted, and himself gave them the means to be so. They headed the processions, but in them marched also men-at-arms and archers. Then came the princes of the blood and the other nobles, nearer the king but never too near. And although from

* But see page 129 below.

Christine's vivid descriptions of him he was obviously the least impressive of them all physically, there was never any doubt who was king. 'I assure you that he did indeed look a prince', she later told his grandson. The people of Paris pressed as close to him as the foot-sergeants who surrounded him would allow. And he would doff his headgear to his subjects 'in sign of love and benignity' — no empty gesture from a king who showed his affection for his people in more substantial ways too (although it is true that later in his reign he began to over-tax them, to pay for his ever-increasing expenditure).

But Christine had chances to see the king much more closely than as a mere spectator on such public occasions. There are indications in her writings that he took much interest in the young daughter of his 'very special, private, and dear counsellor'. No doubt she was permitted to go and see her father in the Hôtel de Saint Pol where there were many things to fascinate a child. There were gardens, for instance, full of flowers of every sort, and hundreds of flowering trees and shrubs which the king had planted, including a great cherry orchard, all of it in charge of a lady gardener, Jeanne la Bouchère. There was an aviary with turtle-doves and nightingales, a vast balustrated basin full of fish and, most exciting of all, a menagerie with no less than ten lions. Although all these things have long since disappeared, the memory of them remains enshrined in the names of the streets that now stand on the site: the *rue des jardins de Saint Paul*, the *rue de la Cerisaie*, the *rue de Beautreillis*, where the vines were trained, and the *rue des Lions*. It must have been in some conversation with the king when she went to play in these delectable places that she was struck by the contrast between his frail form and the beauty of his deep voice. She may even have been admitted to those winter-evening gatherings when stories were read aloud to the king before supper. And there are indications too that she was admitted to the nursery of the two little royal princes.

So the years passed until it became clear to Christine's mother, from the attention that her daughter was beginning to attract, that although she was rather young for it, she was of marriageable age. Her mother may not have believed in formal education but she obviously set store by character, and moral and mental qualities, and these she began to instil into her daughter. Christine describes this in the form of one of those allegories so dear to the Middle Ages, in a continuation of that passage in the *Mutacion de Fortune* already mentioned. In this she relates how her mother, whom she calls Dame Nature for obvious reasons, put on her head a chaplet set with many jewels, which embellished her and made her 'wiser, much more aware and in every way more pleasing'. It would take too long to count all the precious stones, she says, so she will mention only four. The first is discretion, the second consideration, the third retention, which conferred the power of taking in all that one heard, felt or saw and all that the heart conceived. The fourth, a very beautiful stone, was memory, which enabled one to remember all that one had heard or read in science or history. With the gift of these last two her mother was clearly compensating her for her lack of education.

Christine modestly remarks that the fact that she was given these gifts did not mean that she had them in greater measure than others. But she says that she had also the less usual gifts of eloquence and reason, enough to make up for the beauty which, she says in one place, she lacked. And unlike beauty, the virtue of these stones increases in loveliness and strength with the growth of the body. Although perhaps it is true that she was not beautiful, she tells us in another passage that she had a body that was 'pleasant and wholesome with no weakness', and she implies that she had a good complexion too. Certainly the face, small and serious and always easily recognisable, that one sees in the many representations of her in the illuminations of her manuscripts, is not at all without charm.

In any case she was attractive enough to catch the eye of 'many noble knights and rich clerks' who asked for her hand. But her modesty made her think that the honour and love which the king showed her father was as much a cause of this as her own worth. This seems to imply that there were some place-hunters among her suitors. But her father was shrewd enough not to be taken in by them and his choice fell on a young graduate scholar of twenty-four called Etienne de (or du) Castel, born of a noble family in Picardy, who was more virtuous than rich and whom he had long thought of as a son. Christine also had known him from her infancy, and as she says he was beautiful both in face and body it sounds as if their union was that rare thing, a love match. Etienne promised to look after Christine loyally, never to leave her for anyone else, and that they would be 'true friends', a promise that he was to keep faithfully. The king too was pleased, for he gave the young man a post which fell vacant at that time as notary and secretary to himself, with a good salary, and kept him at court as his 'very beloved servitor'. And so in 1379 Christine, at the age of fifteen, became a married woman and left her father's house.

CHAPTER TWO

An Ideal Marriage

GREATLY though Christine had enjoyed her childhood, the next ten years were to be for her a time of deeper happiness still. Although she had implied that her husband was not rich when she married him, the king's generosity obviously so much improved his fortunes that the young couple were able to live in considerable style, since they had four esquires and three demoiselles to look after them and it was altogether a very agreeable household.[1] But it was not these material things that made her so radiantly contented, it was the devoted love of her husband and the care he took of the young girl who had been given into his charge. He was, she tells us, wise, courteous and knowledgeable, but above all loyal, loving and considerate, desiring only that Christine should feel at ease with him. So grateful was she to him for all his love and goodness that she could never praise him enough, and her desire to do so led her to reveal some of the intimate reasons for their happy relationship in a way that is astonishing in the literature of the time. He was so gentle with her on their first night, she says, that he 'did her no outrage' for fear of alarming her; but when it was time to get up next morning, he kissed her a hundred times to reassure her, addressing her as 'sweet friend' and saying that God had created him solely to be of use to her. He liked everything she did and understood and trusted her absolutely, so much so that when, on some later occasion, she was apparently making an excessive fuss of some man-friend, her husband merely laughed and said she might have another friend to amuse herself if she liked, he would not mind. No wonder she wrote with a rare touch of humour, 'God preserve this husband for me, if he gets no worse than he is now, for he has no peer'.[2]

It was well for Christine that her early marriage had brought her so much personal contentment and security, for only a year or two after its celebration the first shadow darkened the hitherto undimmed brightness of her days. In 1380 the always precarious health of the king gave way and he died, aged only forty-four. His death reduced Thomas de Pizan at one stroke from prosperity to comparative poverty, or at least to

25

straitened circumstances. It is true that, only a few months before the king died, he had given him what sounds an important property in Paris,[3] adjoining and perhaps even incorporating (the deed of gift is slightly ambiguous) the Tour Barbeau, which stood on the river bank not far from the Hotel de Sens and marked the southernmost end of the twelfth-century enclosing wall of Philip Augustus. For this Thomas had to pay an annual rent of twelve Parisian pounds. But the king had promised to settle on him and his heirs lands worth five hundred *livres*, and to give him many other goods as well. Unfortunately forgetfulness, and now his untimely death, put an end to any hope of all that. Worse still, Thomas immediately lost the important and well-paid post he had held so close to the king. Thereafter, though he was kept on at court, it was at a greatly reduced and irregularly paid salary. True, the Duke of Burgundy gave him a handsome money gift soon after the king died, and Charles VI a few years later in 1387 gave his 'beloved surgeon', as he called him, another present of 200 francs 'to help him to keep up his state'. But these things were nothing to compare with the constant and lavish generosity of Charles V.

What made matters worse for Thomas was that, in the days of his prosperity he had been much more liberal than his situation warranted, being unable to refuse any request from the poor and forgetting that he had a wife and children for whose future he had to provide. For at some time during the ten years between Christine's arrival in Paris and the death of the king, Thomas and his wife had had two sons. It is not known just when they were born[4] but in any case they must still, at the time of the king's death, have been too young to assist their father financially. Then too, he was getting old. As it was forty years since he had first been appointed a professor in Bologna, he must at the time of the king's death have been at least sixty, which was a good age in those days. The change in his circumstances before long affected his health too and he fell into some long malady that gradually weakened his faculties and made him helpless.

Devoted as she was to her parents, these changes affected Christine deeply. Her personal happiness did not prevent her from sharing her parents' distress and feeling that the blow had fallen on her too. The king's death, she says, 'opened the door to our misfortunes; and though still so young, I passed through it'. Although, looking back long afterwards, she had reason to see this event as presaging later misfortunes, at the time it seems unlikely that she had any need to worry unduly because

26

of the change in their circumstances, for she says that her husband now became the head of the family, from which one may infer that he was able to look after them financially.

What is likely to have distressed Christine far more was to see the father she so deeply admired dismissed from the proud position of authority for which she felt his learning so fitted him, merely, it seemed, because he belonged to the old reign. But there is some reason to doubt whether that learning had ever been as great as Christine would have us suppose, and whether it was not because the late king had himself shared the man's interest in astrology that he set such store by him. Certainly another of the king's councillors, and a much more intellectual one, Philippe de Mézières, referred after the death of Thomas to his poor judgment and the number of times it had misled the king.[5] But none of these things shook Christine's passionate loyalty to her father's memory. She studded her later books with praise of him, writing after his death that there had lived no man of greater understanding in mathematics and astrology and that his fame would live for a hundred years. All the princes, she says, lamented his death because of his wisdom.

Fortunately for Christine, she was still too young and personally happy at that time to be entirely cast down, especially as she had other good reasons then for looking to the future, as well as enjoying her own present life. In 1381 a daughter was born to her and Etienne, followed by a son who seems to have died early or perhaps in childbirth. But in 1385 she had a second son, Jean, of whom she tells us much later. The care of these children (whose births, she said, had caused her great pain) and her duties as a married woman so filled her time and thoughts that once again she neglected the chance of educating herself, which her husband's companionship and help would have afforded her. He was now an important person at court where, she says, he was much loved by the princes, all of whom frequented his office. He was clearly an outstanding young man, and as he was still only in his late twenties, the changes 'customary when the mouth of a powerful man is closed', as Christine puts it, which had affected her father adversely, had on the contrary made an important difference in Etienne's position, since overnight, as it were, from being the bright young secretary and notary of a middle-aged monarch he became the experienced official of a boy half his age.

Charles VI had been born in 1368 and so was only twelve when he came to the throne in 1380. There could not have been a greater contrast than that between him and his father. Where Charles V had been

27

prudent, self-controlled, diplomatic and intellectual, the boy was headstrong and excitable; and not even his tutor Philippe de Mézières, a thinker of considerable standing, had been able to make a good scholar of him. On the contrary he was active, gay, laughter-loving and pleasure-seeking and seemed hardly likely to become a good king. However, this question did not at once arise, for Charles V had decreed that a sovereign should not come of age until he was fourteen. A regency was therefore established, the main members of which were the young king's paternal uncle Philip, Duke of Burgundy, and Louis II, Duke of Bourbon, brother of the late queen. Though he was very fond of his two nephews Bourbon had no real desire for power, so this fell almost entirely into the hands of Philip the Bold who, egged on by his domineering wife, had always nursed an ambition to govern the realm, and was now in a position to gratify it.

It proved to be a far from peaceful regency. There had been a good deal of discontent among the people towards the end of the reign of Charles V, principally because, although he cared for his subjects and was lenient in many things, he taxed them heavily, not only to pay for the expenses of government but also to gratify his passion for building, his love of books and works of art, and his extravagant delight in jewels, fine raiment and the general magnificence of his court. While he lived his personality and qualities held this discontent in check, but on his death it quickly broke out, not only in Paris but throughout the country, where in many places the people rose in rebellion. In 1382 the young king helped his uncle of Burgundy to put down a rebellion at Roosebeke in Flanders and on his return, flushed with victory, for he had personally fought bravely, he punished the rebellious Parisians with many harsh measures. As he was now fourteen he also assumed the royal power. But it was to be six years before he was able to free himself from the tutelage of his uncles.

This he eventually did with the help of his late father's ministers and councillors, two of the chief of whom were Bureau de la Rivière and Jean de Montagu. The former had begun to serve Charles V when he was still only regent. He later became the king's first chamberlain and so loved his master that he was heartbroken when he died. Jean de Montagu had been secretary to Charles V and held the same office under his son until he was made Grand Master of the Household. Christine speaks warmly of him as a wise and loyal man of conscience whom, she says, 'I have reason to remember for he is the father of the poor and the

1 Charles V King of France. A fifteenth-century statue in the Louvre.

Photo Viollet.

II The Louvre as it was rebuilt by Charles V, from the *Très Riches Heures du Duc de Berry*. In the Condé Museum, Chantilly.   *Photo Viollet.*

succour of the needy ... a true friend as I and many others have proved'.[6]
These two, and two more of their colleagues, had been much more
efficient administrators of the affairs of the realm than were the royal
dukes. And in 1388 they persuaded Charles VI that the time had come
to shake off the grip of his uncles, and rule himself with the help of his
ministers, as Charles V had done. As the king was now twenty his
uncles had to accept his decision and for the next four years the Marmousets, as the nobles contemptuously called the ministers because some
of them were of comparatively humble birth, ruled the country well.

Because of her husband's position Christine came to know not only
these officials and others such as Gilles Malet, the royal librarian, and
Guillaume de Tignonville, the Provost of Paris, but many of the ruling
house itself, beginning with the young king and his brother Louis. She
had indeed known them from their infancy and in her allegorical way,
but in a slightly mixed metaphor, she refers to them as 'two little gilded
butterflies, very gracious and of great beauty, who had sprung from the
loins of Charles V'.[7] It seems as if she had even been admitted to their
nursery in their babyhood, for in an uncharacteristically sentimental
passage, with an amusing echo for modern ears, she remarks how sweet
it was to see the child Louis on his knees, his little hands joined before the
image of Our Lady, saying his prayers under the watchful eyes of his
governess Madame de Roussel.[8] During those happy years of Christine's
married life Louis grew into a brilliant prince, handsome, gay and
sportive but still with a devout side, to whose patronage she later owed
much. But the young king Charles VI was even handsomer.

Of the other royals, as they were sometimes called even in those days,
she knew of course Philip of Burgundy, who was always a benevolent
figure to her, especially in later life, as was also the Duke of Berry. For
Louis II, Duke of Bourbon, a man who for once was deservedly called
the good, she has a special admiration and affection. In his young days,
she says, 'he was always, but honourably, amorous, gentle in his
manners, benign in his words, liberal in his gifts'. When he got older 'all
that youthful charm turned into sense and moderation, good counsel,
devotion and charity to . . . all poor people'. He remained a great
admirer of women, helping those who were wronged, 'and of that', says
Christine, 'I may speak from direct experience, for when I needed his
help he never failed me'. Of his handsome son John, Count of Clermont,
Christine says guardedly that he was a man of 'good will, as far as one can
judge, having regard to his youth'.

It seems to have been a predominantly masculine court at that time, for when the queen had died, two years before her husband, none of the great ladies who later roused such fervent admiration in Christine for the members of her sex had yet appeared on the scene. Although Charles VI married his not very attractive German wife Isabeau of Bavaria in 1385 she did not come to Paris until four years later, when she was eighteen and when a fantastic procession was organised to receive her on her way to be crowned at Notre Dame. Christine made the queen's acquaintance soon after that, as also that of other great ladies who accompanied her on that occasion, especially Valentina Visconti, the twenty-one year old daughter of Duke Gian Galeazzo of Milan, who had just become the wife of the king's brother Louis, at that time Duke of Touraine.

Youthful though most of the members of the procession were, probably the youngest was the new Duchess of Berry. Very soon after the death of his first wife, a year or so previously, the duke had become infatuated with Jane, daughter of the Count of Boulogne, who had been living for the past nine years in the care of Count Gaston of Foix, a neighbour but not a friend of his. As the count was not keen on this marriage, Berry asked his nephew the king to help him with the negotiations. The story of this affair was related by Froissart in a vivid account which becomes more racy still in Lord Berners' translation:[9] 'The French king laughed and had good sport with the Duke of Berry, his uncle, because, though so old, he was hot in love, and said to him—Dear uncle, what will you do with so young a maid, she is not twelve years of age, and you are sixty.' But Berry replied, 'If the lady be young, I shall spare her for three or four years, till she be a perfect woman. Well, dear uncle, quoth the king, I fear she will not spare you so long; but since you are so much inclined thereto, I shall aid you as much as I can.' A great deal of aiding was necessary, for the Count of Foix 'saw well the ardent desire the Duke of Berry had, and the hotter he was, the colder was the earl'. But in time he relented, in return for a handsome money payment for all the years he had looked after Jane, and the marriage took place. Froissart ends his story by saying, 'At all this, I, Sir John Froissart, was present'. Incidentally Berry must have appeared a very old man to the twenty-year-old king, who grossly exaggerated his uncle's age, for Berry was then only forty-eight. So perhaps the king thought Jane younger than she was, although she was certainly little more than a child. But there must already have been in her the makings of the spirited and courageous young woman she was soon to show herself, and the sensitive, intelligent woman she later became, to judge by the face of the little statue of her in the cathedral of Bourges.

There is no evidence that Berry's daughter Mary took part in this procession, together with her young step-mother, but Christine must by then have known her for some time, seeing her if not at court perhaps in her father's vast and sumptuous hotel, the Hôtel de Nesles,* one of the few princely houses on the left bank of the Seine, where it occupied a great stretch of land looking across to the Louvre. The proof that Christine knew Mary as a child is that she wrote a *ballade*[10] to her in which she calls her 'ma chiere demoiselle' and addressed her as Countess of Montpensier, the title she bore before her first marriage in 1385 at the age of only twelve or thirteen. Wherever or whenever Christine saw her in those days of her unmarried youth, she was obviously at once struck by the child's quality, for Mary must have been, even in childhood, the exceptional person she afterwards proved herself. In that *ballade* Christine calls her 'noble, pleasant, very gracious and beautiful', as well as 'good, valiant and wise'—many virtues, especially these last, for a child to possess. But there was obviously that in her that made Christine say, in what is probably the first poem she ever wrote, when she herself was still under twenty, that she would like to serve her and hers wherever she might be. And indeed she never thereafter swerved from this devotion.

Another woman who roused Christine's admiration in those early days was not an aristocrat but Marguerite, the young wife of Bureau de la Rivière. An action of hers so impressed Christine that she never forgot it and related it more than twenty years later in one of her most famous books, when Marguerite was still alive. It is such a delightful story, and the sympathy with which Christine tells it is so revelatory of herself that it must be left in her own translated words. 'It happened one day among others that she [Marguerite] was at a very splendid fête given in Paris by the Duke of Anjou, who was then King of Sicily.† There was at that fête a great concourse of noble ladies, knights and gentle folk, all magnificently attired. As this lady, who was young and beautiful, was looking

---

* This huge property, with its gardens and the lofty Tour de Nesles, which long remained a landmark in Paris, filled up the whole space between the modern rue Bonaparte, the rue de Seine, the rue Jacob and the river.[11]

† The *Rue du roi de Sicile* in the Marais now marks the site where then stood the hotel of the Duke of Anjou, always known by his royal title. This episode must have taken place before 1384, since he died in that year.

at the noble chivalry which was there, she realised there was no sign among them of a very notable knight of great renown who lived at that time called messire Emenion de Pommiers. Although he was very old she had never ceased to remember him because of his goodness and valiance. It seemed to her that there could be no finer adornment for such an assembly than notable and renowned men, even if they were old, so she kept asking where that knight was, since he was not present. She was told that he was imprisoned in the Châtelet in Paris because he owed five hundred francs for the frequent journeys he had undertaken when fighting. "Ha!" said the noble lady, "what a great shame it is for this kingdom to allow such a man to be imprisoned for debt for a single hour." Then she took the rich and beautiful gold chaplet which she wore on her head, putting a wreath of periwinkles on her fair hair in its place, and gave it to a messenger saying: "Go and give this chaplet as a pledge for what he owes and let him be quickly freed and come here!" This was done and she was greatly praised.'[12]

But whatever may have been the range of Christine's acquaintance, either with men or women, at court or in any other circle at that time, her pleasure in it paled beside her ever-growing happiness with her husband. What she delighted in above everything else was his daily company which was, she says, so pleasant to her that she felt there could never have been a woman so richly satisfied, for he was able to make of every little amusing trifle something that charmed and delighted her. 'We had so arranged our love and our two hearts', as she put it, 'that we had but one will, closer than brother and sister, whether in joy or in sorrow.'[13] Fortunate as she had been in the choice that had been made for her, marriage in her eyes became, and remained, the ideal state between man and woman, a state in which the man treated his wife as the perfect companion, neither the household drudge which she saw so many women becoming, nor the creature on a pinnacle to be worshipped, which chivalry made of her, while she on her side accepted without question that he was the master of the household. Living daily in such utter contentment, and young as they both were during those ten years of marriage, it looked as though nothing could ever change the felicity of it. But Fortune, the fickle goddess whose capricious ways became later a constant theme with Christine, had other plans for her.

CHAPTER THREE

Persecution and Poetry

ONE day in 1389 Etienne had to accompany the king to Beauvais, presumably on state business although we do not know what it was. It does not seem to have been an important occasion for the king had only a few of his servitors with him. While they were there Etienne was suddenly taken ill. As they were among strangers and had no doctor with them, no one was able to determine what was the matter; and so Etienne died, aged only thirty-four. Christine was of course not with him at the time, and it is not difficult to imagine her state of mind when the news of his death, so unexpected and so unexplained, was brought to her in Paris. She plunged on the instant from what had seemed the secure heights of happiness into an abyss of loneliness where she felt she would always thereafter have to dwell. For although she was only twenty-five, to her it was unthinkable that anyone should ever take the place of the husband she had so loved. No wonder that she so often afterwards lamented that what she called 'all my good days' were over.

'I was so confused with grief', she wrote later, 'that I became a recluse, dull, sad, alone and weary.'[1] So much so that she might well have succumbed to this blow, or merely become a mournful, diminished creature for the rest of her days. But the harsh facts of her practical situation saved her from this, for she realised that, from being a gently nurtured and cherished wife, protected from all the financial side of life, she had become the person on whom not only her own small children depended but her mother and two brothers as well. This was a daunting prospect; but Christine was a woman of spirit and she rose to the occasion, describing in a vivid image how, while she lay wishing for death, Fortune came and turned her into a man.[2] Fear and doubt dropped from her, she felt herself lighter than usual, her voice grew stronger, her body harder and more agile, and she felt capable and bold, able to undertake the struggle necessary to keep her family.

It would have been a cruel struggle in any case, but what made it particularly so was that neither Christine nor her mother could have had much money and she had been left in ignorance of the state of Etienne's financial affairs. 'It is a common habit of married men', she says, 'not to inform their wives entirely of their affairs.' She had already had experience of this universal and enduring truth at the time when her father lost the post that had kept his family in comfort. Small wonder then that she blames the habit in general, saying how bad it is, especially in men whose wives are 'wise and of good governance' and that evil nearly always comes of it.

In Etienne's case there had not been very much to reveal to her, as all he had was his salary and some property which she vaguely knew he had bought as what she calls an inheritance, in other words something that he could eventually leave to her and their children. Although this sounds a simple enough position, such was the attitude of the officials concerned with finance that, as she repeats many times in later works, it was thirteen or fourteen years before she was eventually able to get everything settled. It is a grim and daunting picture that she paints of her unremitting efforts to obtain simple justice. The officials concerned, 'those leeches of fortune' as she calls them, were pastmasters in the art of delay, and seemed to take a malicious pleasure in trying to confuse her and giving ambiguous answers which she was afraid of contradicting. Even when she had obtained a document, verified and passed by the king's *Chambre des Comptes*, concerning a debt due to her from her husband's arrears of salary, those whose duty it was to pay it held up the king's order and instituted a long enquiry. When at last one item was paid, after a six years' delay, the officials reserved a part of the payment for themselves. Whenever one matter was settled, another cropped up that had to be tackled. The date on a form was too old so another one had to be made out. The question of the 'inheritance' proved more difficult still, for it seemed that Etienne had vested the property in the king's hands, on mortgage presumably, so that not only was she not allowed to touch it but had to pay interest on it. Worse still, arrears of such interest were still due, and she had to argue with the 'pitiless man' responsible for this. In such circumstances it was cruelly galling to have to bend the knee to such creatures and to call them Monseigneur.

The mental stress of all this was hard enough to endure, but quite as painful, if not more so, was the physical and moral suffering it entailed. At one time she was pleading and defending herself in no less than four different courts. Sometimes she had to spend whole mornings, frozen with cold in winter, watching for those who had agreed to plead for her to appear, so as to remind them of their promises. So unremitting was the vigilance that was thus forced on her, and so many people was she obliged to frequent, that often her modesty was cruelly wounded by the ribald remarks that began to be made about her, some putting about rumours that she was pursuing these men for other reasons than the true ones—rumours that spread to the whole town, where people began to think she had fallen in love again. One can imagine the pain that such vulgar imputations caused one as single-hearted as she. And if that were not enough, the officials themselves, especially when drunk, often made coarse jokes at her expense, which she had to listen to and pretend not to mind for fear of worsening her situation with them. 'What greater evil can befall the innocent', she says, 'than to hear himself defamed without cause?'

It was all very well to say that she had felt herself becoming as strong as a man to deal with these matters, but she remained very much a timid woman who loathed having to appear in public and run after people all day long. The more she so suffered, the more she tried to put a brave face on things, concealing her grief and trying to laugh. She was proud, too, and took pains not to look shabby, even though her sober cloak, furred with squirrel, 'was not often renewed'. Something that caused her intense shame was an occasion when bailiffs came to distrain on her furniture, taking even small objects that she pathetically calls 'mes chosettes'. Still greater was her shame when, to avoid worse evils still, she was reduced to borrowing. 'How red my face got!' she cries. With her house thus denuded, even temporarily, it was in those years more of a grief than a pleasure to be at home and to see her children and her mother, because then she thought of the contrast between their past happiness and present afflictions. And even at night when she was in her 'beautiful well-made bed'—she took a woman's delight in such things—the thought of her troubles caused her 'great shivers'.

In view of the range of Christine's acquaintance at the court, both among the aristocrats and the officials, it seems strange that none of them helped her in her struggles. She definitely stated later that she found no charity either among the great or the small, although she begged many nobles not indeed to give her financial help, but merely by their support to see that she obtained the help that the law enjoined should be given to widows and orphans. Her heart was so full of indignation about this that she went so far as to write a *ballade*[3] to ease it of its burden. 'Alas', she complains, 'where can poor widows, robbed of their goods,

find consolation, since in France, once the port of safety where exiles and
the wrongly counselled could find refuge, there is now no friendship;
neither the nobles nor the humblest clerks have pity, nor will the princes
listen.' Even prelates and judges will not help and the poor widows
cannot flee for they have nowhere to go. It is certainly a very vehement
ballade and in strong contrast to Christine's later attitude to the great
ones who could help her, when she was always politic and sometimes
even sycophantic.

One explanation of this lack of helpfulness, on the part of Christine's
more influential connections at any rate, was that during that period the
government of the country was in an increasingly unsettled state,
because the king began to suffer more and more from a kind of manic-
depressive condition, in the manic phases of which he was completely
insane. These began with dramatic suddenness one sultry day in August
1392, when, with Berry, Burgundy, Bourbon, Louis of Orleans and a
band of armed followers, the king was on his way to Brittany, to seek a
man who had tried to assassinate one of his favourite councillors and had
then fled to take refuge there. As the day was very hot the company
halted for a while in a forest outside Le Mans. There a ragged man
came up to the king and, seizing the bridle of his horse, warned him to
go no further, telling him he was betrayed. Neither the king nor his
companions took much notice, thinking the poor man's wits were
wandering. Soon afterwards they left the forest and began to cross a wide
sandy plain. It was by then mid-day and the sun was burning hot. Made
drowsy perhaps by the heat, one of the two pages riding behind the king
let fall his master's spear, which in falling struck the steel helmet of his
fellow page. The sudden clatter in the still noon-day heat perhaps reminded the king of the ragged man's words, for suddenly his mind gave
way and, drawing his sword, he turned and made as if to kill the pages,
who fled at the sight of him. The king then rode at his brother of Orleans,
who seeing the mad and murderous look in his eyes, set spurs to his
horse and galloped furiously across the countryside, with the king in hot
pursuit. The rest of the company followed, but it was only when the
king was wearied out that they came up with him. Seeing then that he
could not recognise either his brother or his three uncles, they decided
to abandon the expedition and, putting him in a litter, they carried him
back to Paris. There his physicians said they were not surprised, they had
always known his brains were weak and that one day something like this
might happen.

This first attack, like those which thereafter followed it throughout the rest of his life, was only temporary, but not long after he recovered from it the reckless gaiety which had formerly characterised him became wilder than ever. He had always enjoyed dressing up and disguising himself and one of the occasions when he had done so was during the splendid procession organised for the state entry of Queen Isabeau into Paris in 1389. Then he had put on the clothes of an ordinary citizen and mingled with the crowd, playing the buffoon so wildly that some of them began to strike him and he was in real danger. But the risk then was as nothing compared to that which he ran only six months after the episode at Le Mans. In February 1393 he gave a great ball at the Hôtel de Saint Pol, in the course of which, to entertain the guests, he and five of his friends disguised themselves as savages. They were sewn from head to foot into six specially-made skin-tight linen costumes, which had been smeared with pitch to which flax was stuck to resemble hair. They entered the hall dancing, the king leading them, but the other five linked together. He had given orders that no torches were to come near them, but in the excitement this was forgotten. Moreover it so happened that only at that moment did Louis of Orleans arrive, and in pressing forward to see what was happening, flames from the torches of his followers fell on the group, whose costumes instantly blazed up.

At the sight the queen, who knew that her husband was one of the savages, fainted with fear. In this terrible crisis the only person who seems to have kept her head was the young Jane of Berry, who at once threw the train of her gown round the leading savage, although she did not know who he was, and extinguished the flames. When he told her he was the king, she urged him to go at once to his wife, to reassure her. Only one of his five followers survived that tragic night, by flinging himself into a water butt in a neighbouring room. Two were burnt to death on the spot and the other two died of their burns two days later.

This terrible event, known in French history as the *Bal des Ardents*, or *des Sauvages*, rather surprisingly does not appear to have brought on another of the king's attacks. But it made it abundantly clear that he would never be fit to rule again, and that a regent must be appointed, to take control at any rate during those times when the king, as the chroniclers euphemistically put it, was absent. The obvious choice for this role was Philip of Burgundy, who had already had experience as regent during the king's minority. All might then have gone well if he had been content to keep on those wise councillors, the Marmousets, who had guided the young king so helpfully. But both Burgundy and Berry so despised and hated them, merely because they were not aristocrats, that they at once dismissed them and even threw them into prison. There they remained for two years until the two dukes, no doubt thinking it would be simpler to get rid of them once for all, released them, in order to put them to death. But once again it was Jane of Berry who prevented this cruel deed, for she pleaded with her husband to save the life of one of them, Bureau de la Rivière, whom apparently she knew better than the others. Was she perhaps a friend of his young wife, Marguerite, who had spoken out so boldly on behalf of the old knight at the Duke of Anjou's ball? It seems not unlikely, for their characters, which made them both particular favourites of Christine's, were obviously akin. Fortunately for the Marmousets, Jane's doting elderly husband could obviously refuse her nothing, and because of her intercession, since one could not be pardoned without the others, all were saved from death and sent instead into exile.

Without them to keep him in check Philip of Burgundy might then have become a tyrant, for he had grown into a forceful character, and his wife was a dominating personality who was continually urging him to resist the claims of his nephew Louis. Now a young man of twenty-three, the latter had recently been given by the king the important duchy of Orleans, with its wide lands, in place of Touraine, so that he was a considerable landowner in the countryside as well as in Paris, where he had many fine houses. He understandably felt that, as he was nearer in blood to the king than his uncle Philip, it was for him to govern in his place. Moreover as time went on he was relatively free to pursue his ambitions because in 1396 his noble young wife Valentina, whose calm and gentle disposition had made her the only person who could soothe the poor king in his attacks of madness, was exiled to her husband's country estates because of jealous fears, either on the part of Queen Isabeau, or of Burgundy, that she might exercise too much influence over the king on behalf of her husband.

If all these personages at court were too much taken up with their intrigues to pay much heed to Christine, she had other friends who were not. They too had no practical or financial help to give her. Instead they gave her something else, something which is rarely acceptable, but which in her case produced miraculous results, and indeed may be said to have altered her whole life: this was advice. They suggested that, instead of sitting grieving over her lost love in silence, during such intervals at home as her pursuit of justice allowed her, she should try to put into verse the feelings that so totally absorbed her heart—an early example of writing as a therapeutic measure. She felt doubtful of her ability to do as they suggested. But after all she had already written that *ballade* to the little Mary of Berry, and also her *ballade* of complaints against all those who had refused to help her. And perhaps it was a sight of this last which had put the idea in the heads of her friends.

So she allowed herself to be persuaded and set to work to pour out all her pent-up love, past happiness and present sorrow in a series of twenty *ballades*[4] that are not only technically skilful but memorable for the poignant simplicity and sincerity of the emotions they express. It is from some of these that we know of her happy childhood and how her mother and nurse used to comfort and spoil her. Now that her 'sweet friend' has left her '*seulete*'—her favourite version of the word *seule*—shut up in her room, how can she do other than weep and sigh, remembering how she had known him since infancy and first youth. Now that he is no longer there, she does not know how to manage, for she is still young and not very clever. In one poem, which must have been written in 1394, she says that it is now five years since she lost him, and since then she has been so hurt that she begs Death to write her name in his book. Sometimes she trembles like a leaf, so great is her pain, and she thinks of killing herself. In the last of the series she says that it is now ten years since her heart felt joyful; and she has no more desire to make a friend or to love.

Having thus purged her heart of some of its bitter regrets and discovered that she had the gift of writing beautiful, simple love poems, it is almost as if she could not stop. For she then went on to compose more and more until she has written no less than a hundred.[5] In them she invents an imaginary love affair and draws on either her own experience or her intuitive knowledge of all the emotions that beset the hearts of lovers, both men and women. She describes their joys, but also their occasional doubts and fears, such as those of a woman when her loved one has to travel to other countries, sometimes for long periods. When she has no news she fears he may have forgotten her, or loves another, and so on his return she greets him with a momentary coldness, which puzzles and distresses him since he had thought of none but her.

All these emotions are portrayed with such vividness and have such a ring of truth about them that her friends, when they saw them, began to wonder whether perhaps the affair she describes was altogether imaginary. And indeed it is almost as if Christine were taking a deliberate and amused pleasure in leading them on and making them think so. For one thing she writes in the first person, so that there is no break in the tone of these poems and that of the earlier ones. In the first of the new series, she says that a charming man has fallen in love with her and tells her so with such gentle sighs that she has not the heart to turn him away, especially as she is attracted to him. So she accepts him and then goes on to say that his goodness has dried up all her former grief and that Fortune has become kind to her again. In another *ballade* she tells him that he must forgive her if she will not always speak to him, for she has to be careful since many people are spying on her.

Most misleading of all is a *ballade* in which she says that her beloved 'friend' has gone to England and she does not know when she will see him again. Now in 1397, not long after the marriage of Richard II to the princess Isabelle, the seven-year old daughter of Charles VI, the Earl of Salisbury,* a faithful supporter of Richard's, happened to be in Paris, perhaps on some business arising from this marriage. This 'gracious knight', as Christine calls him, who loved poetry and was himself a poet made Christine's acquaintance during his visit and became a great admirer of her work—an admiration that quickly led to a still closer connection between them, a connection that may have played its part in fostering her friends' suspicions.

But although Christine may have derived a passing amusement from misleading her friends, she had no wish to keep up a fiction that, however innocent, she might have felt was dishonouring her one and only love. So in the hundredth *ballade*, although she says she has written them with real feeling, in order to keep her promise to those who so warmly urged her, she begs those who read them now, or will read them hereafter, to take them merely as entertainment and not to put wrong interpretations on them. Indeed, already in the fiftieth she had said that these love poems were not personal, 'for in truth my labours are elsewhere'. Finally she remarks that she has not written them to gain merit, nor for any payment, although in her small way she has tried to make them worthy of renown.

These *ballades*, her first attempts at writing, were in fact too slight a matter to be turned to any financial account at that time. In any case her

---

* Salisbury, who had been Sir John Montagu, had succeeded his uncle as Earl of Salisbury in June 1397.

need for money in those closing years of the century must have been less pressing than at the beginning of her widowhood. That endless waiting upon the financial authorities to obtain the payments due to her from her husband's estate must by then have borne some fruit; and she tells us that one of the treasurers had come to her aid in the matter. In 1392 she sold the castle of Mémorant, and some other lands which her father had bought, to Philippe de Mézières,[6] the late king's closest and most respected councillor, although one wonders why he should have wanted them, for he was then nearly seventy years old and had already retired to the Convent of the Celestines in Paris, where he spent the last twenty years of his life. Perhaps he bought them to help Christine.

By 1394 also she had fewer people to keep, for her two brothers, Paolo and Aghinolfo, not having been able to make a living in Paris, had by then returned to Italy, where their father had left them his property.[7] They were good men and devoted to their mother and sister, who both missed them greatly, Christine says, particularly when they saw others happy with their relations around them, and thought how far away from all theirs they were. Christine does however refer to one or two 'poor relations' who were a charge upon her, and there is a reference to a poor niece.* But who she could have been, unless one of the brothers had married and left his daughter with Christine when he returned to Italy, we do not know.

If Christine missed her two brothers, she must still more have missed her children, for they had turned out well and were 'beautiful and gracious, of good discretion, and good behaviour, and God-fearing'. In fact so God-fearing was the eldest of them, her daughter, whose name she never tells us, that of her own free will, and against her mother's wish—for the child was in the flower of her youth and extremely beautiful—she had decided to take the veil at the famous Dominican Abbey of Poissy, which lay about twenty miles to the west of Paris, close to the forest of Saint Germain-en-Laye. In that contemplative life she bore herself with such devotion that when Christine was told of it she felt comforted. The young nun also wrote often to her mother, letters wishing that she too could learn to hate the world. Although Christine had apparently no inclination, at any rate at that time, to follow her daughter's example, the letters from this young and innocent creature were, she says, a great consolation to her.

* See page 120 below.

Of her two sons, the younger appears to have died early, for except for the fact of his birth she never thereafter mentioned him. The second, Jean, had been a good scholar from his youth, especially gifted in grammar, rhetoric and the language of poetry, and with a good singing voice. With all these qualities he had caught the eye of the Earl of Salisbury, during that visit of his to Paris in 1397; and he had suggested to Christine that she should let him take the child to England to be brought up in his household with his own son, a boy of the same age. This chance of a training in a noble household was obviously too good to be refused, and so in 1397 at the age of thirteen the boy left home with what his mother must have hoped would be a notable career before him.

It was very probably at this time that Christine wrote her *Enseigne-mens Moraux*,[8] which she headed 'Les Enseignemens que je Christine donne a Jean de Castel, mon fils'. This is a poem of a hundred and thirteen stanzas, each of four lines, of a kind that was very popular in the Middle Ages. The moral precepts were rarely original, being taken for the most part either from ancient authors or from popular proverbs and sayings, and in this short work Christine is no more distinguished than her predecessors. She begins by saying that, as she has no great treasure with which to enrich her son, she gives him these teachings. But only one or two of her pieces of advice were suitable for the boy he then was, such as when she counsels him not to make faces in speaking. The greater number seem meant for his guidance when he should be grown up, and perhaps have married and become a father, when she may have presumed that he would still be living in England. She then does occasionally reveal something of her own views and preoccupations. It is very much Christine, for example, who counsels him, if he wishes to live chastely, not to read either Ovid's *Art of Love*, or the *Roman de la Rose*, two books in which, as she was soon to show, she was at that time much absorbed. She shows her own hand too when she advises him not to let his daughters be idle and to make his sons learn at school. It is more important to introduce your children to learning than to strive to obtain possessions and land to leave them. Except for these one or two personal-sounding pieces of advice the poem is of no great interest or quality and a kind of sequel she wrote to it, entitled *Proverbes moraux*,[9] is frankly dull.

In 1399 Salisbury visited Paris again, his mission this time being to frustrate a marriage rather than to further one. Henry, Earl of Derby, after he had been exiled from England by Richard II, had settled in

Paris and been made much of by the French king and court, so much so
that Charles VI suggested he should marry his cousin Mary of Berry,
whose first two husbands had both died. Salisbury represented to Charles
that Richard would take such a French alliance for his opponent ill and
the arrangements were consequently broken off, no doubt to the great
relief of Mary, whose heart was already deeply engaged elsewhere.
Christine does not mention seeing Salisbury at this time, although as she
was close both to him and to Mary of Berry, it is almost impossible that
she should not have done, if only to get news of her son Jean.

Now that she no longer had responsibility either for her brothers or
her children, Christine had of course much more time for her writing.
The success of those first *ballades* obviously encouraged her to continue
writing lyric poetry, which she did at intervals for some years to come.
In 1392 Eustache Deschamps, one of the outstanding poets of the time
and indeed of the Middle Ages, had written a treatise on the poetic art
called *L'Art de Dicter*. In it he described all the popular forms of lyric
poetry: the *ballade*, the *rondeau*, the *lay*, *virelay*, *complainte* and so on,
with all the variants in the way of metre and rhyme that are possible in
them; and he wrote an immense number of such poems himself,
apparently with great facility. As Christine knew him and was later to
write to him, it was very likely Deschamps who inspired her to try her
hand at some of those other verse-forms too, for she said later that she
seriously studied the work of other poets. But she had not the necessary
lightness of touch for such elegant trifles as the *lay* and the *virelay*. Hers
are artificial and even dull, the work of someone more concerned to try
her hand at a particular metre, rather than to try and capture a passing
emotion or fancy, as Deschamps could.

The *rondeau* was a different matter, and her *rondeaux* and later
ballades are evidence of how rapidly she acquired poetic skill, and became
so at home in her verse that she was able to write poems that are worthy
to compare not only with those of Eustache Deschamps but with the
graceful and accomplished *ballades* of Charles d'Orléans, who indeed
sometimes seems to echo some of her sentiments and expressions. There
are sixty-nine *rondeaux*,[10] the first of them written in 1396, for she says
in it that her sorrow has lasted seven years. In the first seven her subject
is still the loss of her husband, which has left her alone 'like a turtle dove
without its companion, or a sheep without a shepherd'. Another begins
'I am a widow, alone and dressed in black' and in another she says 'I
know not how I can bear it'. But after a little of this she decides that

43

perhaps she has written enough in this vein and must at least pretend to be gay. So she returns to the theme of her imaginary lover.

Her later *ballades*[11] are interesting in a different way from the *rondeaux* because they are more varied in subject and in some of them Christine's lifelong preoccupations begin to appear. Indeed, already in the first hundred there were a few such. We see for instance the first signs of her concern for the well-being of the country, which later became such an ardent patriotism, in a *ballade* in which she complains of the ambitious and greedy struggle of some nobles, who no longer love honour as in former times but think only of seizing things for themselves and so harm the poor. In another she laments the state to which this has brought France and goes so far as to see in the illness of 'our good king' a kind of penance for the evils in his kingdom. Christine the moralist makes her appearance in a *ballade* praising the virtues of loyalty and especially goodness, for without goodness, beauty and noble rank are worthless. Anyone who has acquired honour by goodness has treasure enough, 'for whoever is good must be called rich'.

More important than Christine the moralist, and just as important as Christine the patriot, was Christine the upholder of the cause of women, both those who are weak and have none to fight for them, and those who are strong but whose abilities she felt were not sufficiently appreciated, and who are still treated as inferior human beings because they are women. It is as a defender of the former that she really appears for the first time in these poems. It is almost as if, after spending so much time and eloquence in lamenting her own misfortunes, she suddenly realised that she was not alone in her suffering and that there were other women as wretched as she. So she calls on all knights to protect the rights of women and revenge poor widows and maidens against extortioners, and against men who delight in speaking ill of them.

But the time was soon to come when merely to touch on a theme of such importance to her in a lyric or two, for more or less private circulation, was clearly not enough. Or it may be that the reception given to those *ballades* by some of her women friends inspired her to further flights on the subject in a more important way. But what form should such a further flight take? A spur was needed and, as so often happens when the mind is full of a subject, one was quickly found.

CHAPTER FOUR

The Writer Emerges

THAT spur Christine found in the most famous poem of the Middle Ages, the *Roman de la Rose*. In the fiftieth of her *Cent Ballades*, in begging her readers not to think that she herself was the subject of her love poems, she had mysteriously said 'For in truth my labours are elsewhere', meaning presumably that she had more serious work on hand than falling in love again and writing verse about it. That serious work was very probably her attempt to educate herself, in order to fill that gap in her upbringing which she had always so deplored. If this were so, the reading on which she embarked while her life was still made so difficult because of her poverty, and when she was no longer in her first youth, may well have seemed a labour rather than the delight which it became later. And it must have been indeed an effort when she began to study, as she now did, that enormous poem, over 21,000 lines long, the *Roman de la Rose*, which remained required reading, for anyone with any claim to be thought educated, for two or three hundred years after its composition in the thirteenth century, but which the obsolescence of its language makes it difficult for any but scholars to read today.

Even for Christine some of it must have been heavy going, after the first short part of the poem in which Guillaume de Lorris relates a dream in which he penetrated into a closed garden where he found a perfect Rose in bud, with which he fell desperately in love. Various allegorical personages: the God of Love himself, Fair Welcome, Frankness and Pity, conspired to help him, but Danger, Evil Tongue and Even Reason warned him against the pursuit of his heart's desire to win the Rose, who represents of course an exquisite virgin. This short section ends when Jealousy has Fair Welcome and the Rose, too, imprisoned in a castle. When, forty years after the death of Lorris, Jean de Meun took up the unfinished poem, he continued the love-story spasmodically; but he interspersed it with endless references and examples from ancient history and mythology, so that what had been a fresh and simple story becomes a long-drawn-out and rather wearisome allegorical intrigue. Quite apart from this are the many digressions, unconnected with the story and quoting authorities of all kinds, covering such subjects as the endless debate on predestination and free will, the nature of dreams, alchemy and the transmutation of metals, astronomy and all the heavenly bodies, natural phenomena such as meteors, comets, floods and the rainbow, the properties of mirrors and glasses—a veritable compendium of the knowledge and beliefs of the Middle Ages. If Christine read it all, as she probably did for she was both thorough and persistent, she would certainly have brought herself abreast of the accepted learning of her contemporaries.

But it was not these matters that at first engaged her attention so much as the indictment of women for which de Meun uses the love-story as a peg. In one of his most cynical passages, which he puts into the mouth of an allegorical personage, an old woman whom he simply calls La Vieille, he describes all the tricks and artifices, both in their appearance and their behaviour, which he says women use to deceive and ensnare men. He implies that this is true of all women when he begs honest ones not to blame him for what he has said, he has only done it so that they may learn to know themselves better. He then exonerates himself by saying that in any case he is only repeating what ancient authors have said: Virgil for instance, who thinks all women are capricious and changeable, Solomon, who says they have vicious dispositions, and Livy, who finds them so credulous and naive that only flattery will serve. Often the Scriptures proclaim that all feminine vice springs from avarice. One of his criticisms that galled Christine most was that women cannot keep secrets and even a loyal wife will betray the confidence of her husband. It is true that de Meun does mention a few cases of chaste and faithful women, such as Dido and Oenone, and blames the fickle men who deserted them, saying he could name a thousand such; but such brief references are few compared with the long passages of denunciation on which he spent much more eloquence.

It is not surprising that these sweeping and one-sided generalisations roused Christine's indignation, both as a woman who herself could not have been said to have deserved any of de Meun's criticisms, and on behalf of many of her feminine acquaintance for whose conduct and virtues she had such admiration. Then too the poet's picture of men as the victims of these rapacious creatures hardly accorded with the impressions she had received. It may be that she was too serious-minded to take such things lightly or just shrug them off. Instead she burned to

redress the balance; and since writing had now become her way of
expressing her feelings, she found a literary framework in which to
clothe them, and produced her first sustained piece of work, a poem
called *L'Epistre au Dieu d'Amours*.[1]*

This opens with Cupid, the God of Love, telling his assembled loyal
subjects that he has received complaints from women of all degrees,
humbly asking his help because every day they suffer at the hands of
disloyal men all kinds of outrages, from extortion to blame and betrayal.
You can see men prancing about the streets on horseback, spurring their
steeds and showing off on their way to feasts. Some who pretend to be
loyal lovers seduce simple and ignorant women into loving them and
then mock them for giving in too soon; others tell their friends in taverns
intimate details about them. Even nobles in the courts of 'our lords the
dukes' indulge in such talk round the fire in the evenings.

After these remarks, clearly based on what she had seen and heard for
herself, Christine turns to what had induced her to write the poem:
those writers who have revelled in traducing women. There was of
course a whole world of such literature, both ancient and medieval, as de
Meun had indicated, for stories of false, inconstant or evil women had
naturally always been a much more popular theme than those of the
chaste and virtuous, as making for livelier reading. But probably
Christine was not yet widely enough read to know much of this literature, and so she begins with an example she certainly had read, Ovid's
Art of Love, which she thinks should rather be called the *Art of Great
Deceit*, since it teaches how to trick women but not how to love well—
the underlying assumption of it being, of course, that women are light
enough to be easily deceived. She makes a shrewd hit when she says, if
women are indeed as light and fickle as such writers say, what need to
take such pains to deceive them? She then turns to Jean de Meun who,
in the *Roman de la Rose*, teaches the same art of deceit at great length.
What a long and difficult business he makes, she says, merely of how to
deceive a virgin. But curiously enough, she does not refer to those
passages to which she might much more legitimately have taken
exception, in which he charges women of being themselves the
deceivers.

Having shot these small and on the whole rather feeble bolts, she

---

* A paraphrase of this poem was made three years later, in 1402, by the poet
Thomas Hoccleve, pupil of Chaucer, with the title *The Letter of Cupid*.

stands up for her sex herself, and in the arguments she uses to defend women reveals some of her qualities both of common sense and ingeniosity. If there are some bad women, must the whole sex be blamed because of them? There were even some bad angels, but should one therefore call all angels bad? Woman, she replies, may even be called superior to man since God created her not out of the clay of the earth but out of the body of the man 'the most noble of earthly things'. God had honoured all women in choosing to be born of one. When Jesus was dead he was abandoned by all save the women. The hearts of women are not naturally inclined to cruelty. They do not kill or wound others, disinherit them, make false contracts or cause harm to the kingdom, for they are by nature pitiful, timid, humble, gentle and charitable.[2] These arguments, supposedly addressed to the God of Love, convinced him that the complaints he had received were justified, for the poem ends by his commending his household to punish all who have defamed women and banish them from his court. This order is 'given in our great palace of the air', on the solemn feast of May when lovers make their requests—'in the year of grace one thousand three hundred and ninety nine'.

This first of Christine's longer poems marks a significant stage in her development. To mention Jean de Meun critically was an extraordinarily courageous thing for anyone to do at a time when his great poem— for it is a great poem—was universally considered beyond reproach, and had never been questioned before. That the critic was a comparatively unknown woman writer made the matter more astonishing still. Then, slight though this first gesture of defiance was, to have dared to make it obviously emboldened Christine to return to the attack, which she was to do three years later, this time using much heavier guns, in a way that made her a main protagonist in one of the most famous literary quarrels of the Middle Ages, and brought her name before a wider public than she had previously known.

But before this happened she found that she was not the sole defender of her sex, for there had come to the aid of women, in quite a different way, one of the most famous soldiers of the time, Jean le Meingre, called Boucicaut. A man three years younger than Christine, he had from the age of sixteen been taking part in various European campaigns and had so distinguished himself that he was made a Marshal of France. But his greatest wish was to fight against the Turk and so he took part in that crusade that suffered a major defeat at Nicopolis in

1396, in the course of which he was taken captive and remained in prison for eight months before he was ransomed.

Whether or not it was that during those months in captivity Boucicaut had had time to wonder how his wife was faring in his absence, not to mention the wives of his fellow prisoners, on his return in 1399 he decided to found an order of chivalry whose members would pledge themselves to 'succour all ladies and maidens of noble lineage'. This Order, which he called *L'Ecu Vert à la Dame Blanche*,[3] by a curious coincidence came into being on April 11th, 1399, just three weeks before Christine finished her poem. She greeted it, as one would imagine, with enthusiasm. Although its aims were limited to a particular category of women, to which she herself did not belong, the mere idea that one of the nobles should be thinking of defending women against those who would harm them was a comfort and encouragement to her.

There were thirteen members of the new Order, which was founded 'because powerful men had robbed women of their lands'. Christine names three of these members in one of her subsequent *ballades*,[4] in which she urges ladies and young girls to pray for all the knights of the Green Buckler. Rather strangely she wrote no *ballade* to Boucicaut himself, but there are two to one of the chief members of his Order, Charles, the young Lord of Albret, a cousin of the king. It would appear from these that she had clearly admired him as a champion of women even before he joined the Order, for the poems are full of praise for the way he had comforted them in adversity, harming them neither in deeds nor words and combating those who do so. Now that he is armed to that end, as a knight of Boucicaut's Order, she prays God to help him sustain their rights.

These *ballades* to Charles of Albret, the first Christine had addressed to anyone by name, show that she had now reached a social position where she could fittingly again approach some of the nobles she had known in her happier days. To her the most important of these at that time was Louis, Duke of Orleans. By the turn of the century he had become not only a great political force in the country but a rich and powerful prince. In addition he was physically most attractive, especially to women, and gifted in many ways, as Christine makes clear in a vivid description of him in one of her later works.[5] To everyone he was courteous and moderate in his speech, being gifted with a natural eloquence; and he was especially amiable to anyone who had need of him, as she found herself. For it so happened that on one occasion she had to ask his help. Being shown into his presence, presumably with other applicants, she had to wait more than an hour for her turn. During that time she took great pleasure in watching his face and admiring the methodical way in which he despatched the affairs he had to attend to. She noticed too how gentle he was with those who were ill at ease or timid in his presence. When her turn came he called her and quickly granted her request.

Christine does not tell us what the request was that Louis on this occasion so quickly granted. But she was less successful when she interceded with him on behalf of her son Jean. The fair future that had seemed to be opening for him when he was taken to England by the Earl of Salisbury in 1397 had come to a tragic end just over two years later, when the Earl was beheaded in January 1399 for his part in a conspiracy to murder Henry IV in revenge for the death of Richard II, whose faithful follower Salisbury had always been. So the boy Jean, then fifteen, was left without a patron. But the new king, Henry IV, rather surprisingly showed himself in a most humane light to this young charge of his late enemy; and Christine's account of what he did affords an interesting example of how contemporary literature can throw light on a historical character. It seems that some of the poems that Christine had sent to please Salisbury were brought to Henry's notice and he was so impressed by them that, for his mother's sake, he took the boy into his own court and made much of him. What was more, he sent two of his heralds, Lancaster and Falcon, to France to beg Christine to go herself to England, offering to provide generously for her.[6] These offers did not tempt her either for her son or herself, for she says that she 'could not believe that so disloyal a man would turn out well'—obviously her connection with Salisbury had predisposed her in Richard's favour. But as she did not want to offend the king by refusing outright she appeared to temporise, asking him first to send her son back to France as she wanted to see him—a move that she wryly says cost her a gift of some of her books. When she got Jean back she presumably refused the king's invitation, for she kept the boy with her, though fearing lest the contrast with her humble home-life might make him wish to return to the state in which he had recently lived.

It must have been some such fear that made her decide that the best course for the boy would be if some great prince in France would take him into his household, as Salisbury had done. To this end she sent Louis of Orleans a *ballade* in which she offered him 'the thing she holds dearest in the world', her son Jean who, 'small though he is, desires to serve you.'[7] But apparently this request of Christine's was not granted for she says that the boy's youthful gifts were not enough to let him make any impression at Louis' court. So for the time being he remained at home at her charge until, a few years later, she was to find him the kind of position she wanted for him with another great noble.

As her son and his future were evidently much on her mind at this time, it is more than likely that it was for him that she then wrote a more elaborate version of the moral guidance that she had previously sent him. This time she does not expressly say that it was written for him, but the fact that she underlines that it was for someone of fifteen, in the fanciful title which she gave it, *Lepistre Othea la deesse, que elle envoya a Hector de Troie quand il estoit an laage de quinze ans*, would seem to indicate that Jean was the boy intended, since there was no one among the sons of the nobles she knew who was that age in 1400, which is considered to be the date of the work.[8]

It is a curious book. It gives the impression that its aim was not so much to give advice as partly to set forth a few of her most cherished views and partly to utilise some of the knowledge that she had enjoyed gleaning in her recent attempts to educate herself. The book consists of a hundred short so-called 'texts' in rhyme, each concerned with a virtue or a vice, often embodied in some mythical character or story. These Christine puts into the mouth of her goddess of prudence or wisdom, to whom she gives the name Othea,[9] who counsels the boy Hector either to emulate or avoid them. Some are merely just pieces of sensible advice, often slightly comic, as when she advises him not to try and run faster than Atalanta *'car plus que toy grant talent a'* (a kind of rhyme much favoured by Christine) since Atalanta was, after all, a professional! Christine herself, in her own name, then commented on these 'texts' in prose 'glosses and allegories' drawing lessons from them and supplementing her own views with quotations from the Bible, the Fathers and the ancient philosophers, and allusions to the tale of Troy, Greek mythology and ancient history. Although this suggests that it is the work of an immensely well-read and learned writer, in fact much of this 'learning' Christine had probably taken from anthologies of one sort or another, for such borrowing was at that time a universal practice, with no stigma of plagiarism attached to it.[10]

Although to modern readers *Othea* is one of the least palatable of Christine's works, in her own day it was much admired and was in fact one of the only four of her books to be printed in her own country in the century of her death.[11] Christine must have realised its appeal, for she quickly devised a method of making it as widely known as she possibly could and at the same time causing it to earn for her the money she always badly needed. She dedicated the first copy to Louis of Orleans, who, in addition to being a powerful prince and a great social success, was also a very cultivated man and a patron of letters—he was having a translation of the Bible, the first ever done into French, made for him at that time. As, like the other Valois princes, he was engaged in building up a library, no doubt he was happy to receive a copy of this latest work of Christine's, and he would certainly have given her a handsome money present for it, as the custom was. She then proceeded to have other copies made, of which we know that one was for the king and one each for the Dukes of Burgundy and Berry, each with an appropriate dedicatory poem; and no doubt she received a suitable recompense in each case, as there is plenty of evidence that she did on similar occasions later in her life.

In an age when writing was hardly a paying proposition, even for a man, Christine had certainly hit upon a brilliant method of living by her pen and one for whose apparent originality she must be given full credit. A proof of the zeal with which she put it into practice is the unusually large number of manuscripts of her works that are now scattered about in the great libraries of Europe.[12] There are for instance no less than forty-eight manuscripts of *Othea*, one of the most beautiful having no less than one hundred full-page illustrations.[13] Some of these were prepared under her supervision for we know, from a passage in one of her most famous later books, that Christine took much interest in the illuminators of manuscripts, especially in one who was a woman.*

Having succeeded so well with this book, Christine pursued the same tactics with others, though not perhaps to the same extent as she had with *Othea*. But in time it became unnecessary for her to do her own publicity in this way, for she tells us that the princes to whom she gave her books not only received them joyfully but talked about them everywhere and sent them to their fellow princes in foreign lands as a novelty in being written by a woman and inspired by her womanly feelings. They were obviously eagerly read everywhere, since Christine quotes a proverb as saying, 'New things please'. Christine, with her gifts, was certainly a 'new thing' and there is no doubt that she was beginning to please.

* See pages 129, 130 below.

One of the great foreign princes who learnt of her work in this way was Gian Galeazzo, the first Duke of Milan. This was hardly surprising for he was the father of Valentina, wife of Louis of Orleans, one of the ladies whom Christine most admired; and we know that she on her side admired Christine's books, some of which are in the inventory of her library. The duke was so impressed with those that he saw that he copied the example of Henry IV of England, and sent Christine ambassadors begging her to go and live at his court. It seems that she seriously considered this offer, for she says 'Not that I would lightly have thought of leaving France, for certain reasons, even though it [i.e. Italy] was my native country'. But not long afterwards, the need to decide was taken from her, for the Duke of Milan died in 1402 and so Christine remained in France for the rest of her life.

CHAPTER FIVE

Lovers' Debates

ONE of those reasons which made Christine reluctant to leave France at that time must have been her children. Not only was she, as we know, much concerned with her son's future (for Milan's offer did not include him as Henry IV's had done); she did not forget her daughter, the young nun who had taken the veil at Poissy. This great royal nunnery, one of the most famous of the time, had been founded by Philip the Fair in 1304 and was dedicated to Saint Louis, who had just then been canonised. Although always called an abbey it was in reality a priory; and it was customary for the prioress to be of noble, and sometimes royal, blood. At the time when Christine's daughter took the veil the Prioress was Mary of Bourbon, sister of Queen Jane, the wife of Charles V, and of Christine's friend and helper, Louis II, Duke of Bourbon. In spite of the girl's happiness in the religious life, which she had herself chosen, she missed her mother greatly, and Christine on her side longed to see again the daughter who was so close to her and in whom she said 'is my desire'.

Accordingly, one morning in the spring of 1400 she decided to go and visit her in her convent; and the poem which she wrote on her return, *Le Livre du Dit de Poissy*,[1] is perhaps the freshest and most spontaneous of all her books. The visit took place, she says, one Monday in April—a precision that gives a wonderful actuality to the whole expedition; and she adds that it was the sweetest morning they had had that year. She took with her a band of young men and women, as she was determined to make the visit a happy occasion. Everyone was in the right mood—none was silent and none spoke sharply, she says—and her description of their ride is so vivid and poetical that it calls to mind that enchanting picture of a May-day cavalcade in the Duke of Berry's *Très Riches Heures*. The dew was glittering on the grass, she says, and the fields through which they rode were already starred with wild flowers. When their route took them along the Seine the shepherds guarding their flocks in the meadows on its banks were making themselves wreaths of wild flowers. They enlivened their journey by inventing and playing all sorts of diverting

games, and by singing. Their songs mingled with those of the many
birds, especially of the nightingales, in the forest of Saint-Germain, so
that the whole air resounded. Soon after they emerged from the forest
they reached Poissy, which lies close to its edge.

They had not dallied too long on their journey, as Christine had
promised to be at the abbey at a certain time. After this charming prologue, the poem enters into what is by far its most interesting section: a
detailed description of life in a religious house, such as is hardly to be
found elsewhere except in books of conventual rules; and this is enlivened by Christine's account of the party's overnight stay in the town of
Poissy. Before they reached the entrance gate, between its two flanking
towers which are all that remains of the vast abbey to-day, they relaxed a
little and changed into their best clothes. Inside they were received in the
parlour by what Christine calls 'the ladies', who presumably lived retired
lives there but were not nuns, since they wore not habits but simple
clothes and head-dresses. There the daughter whom, she says, 'I love so
much and hold so dear' came and knelt down before her. Her mother
'kissed her sweet and tender face', after which they went hand in hand
into the great convent church to give praise to God and to hear Mass.
After the service the ladies asked them to stay to lunch; but first the
Prioress Mary of Bourbon begged them to go and see her in the beautiful
royal hostel. While they were there the 'young and tender' princess
Mary of France, a daughter of King Charles VI came in. She was then
only eight years old and had taken the veil there when she was only five.
The Prioress told them how the priory was run and of the austere lives
of the nuns, who slept in their clothes on hard mattresses, were beaten if
they did not rise for Matins, and as a rule saw their visitors only through
iron grilles. So obviously a great exception had been made for Christine's
daughter.

No such austerity reigned at the lunch with the ladies, where the nuns
served them with wine and meats in gold and silver vessels. After the
meal they returned to thank the Prioress, and then the ladies showed
them their own pleasant cloister with pretty rooms opening off it and
their dormitories in which they had beautiful beds. There was a
splendid pine tree growing in the middle of the cloister. Then the nuns
insisted on taking them round the grounds, full of fruit-trees, enclosed
by a high wall whose line one can still trace. In that vast extent there was
an enclosure too where horned deer, hares and rabbits lived, and two
fishponds, one of which remains to-day. But by then it was getting near

to the nuns' dinner-time, and as any nun who was late for this lost her share and was severely blamed, the moment had obviously come to take their leave. But Christine's daughter, who all this time had been holding her mother's hand, begged her to stay in Poissy overnight and to return after dinner that night to see them again.

Christine and her party found some lodgings where they had a light dinner, though after the lavish lunch they did not want to eat much. So they rested and talked until they were sent for again. It was unusual for visitors to be allowed in the priory twice in one day, but the prioress made an exception in their case and they were able to sit in the gardens and talk with the nuns of holy matters until it was time to go. Christine wept when she said farewell to her daughter, and her friends tried to cheer her by talking of other things as they returned to their hostelry, where supper was served to them in the garden under trellises. The prioress had sent them some of her good wine in gilded pots, and 'the ladies' had also sent some beautifully light, sweet tarts, with apples and pears.

Their conversation as they ate turned on different things, and among others on such French knights as were renowned for 'goodness, sense, valour and grace'. Among these was mentioned Jean de Werchin, Seneschal of Hainault, than whom, it was generally agreed, there was no better knight in France, nor a better lover. On hearing this Christine, who knew he admired her work since he had once asked her to write a poem for him, determined to dedicate to him the one she was already planning to write on the subject of that day's doings. One of the company offered to take it to him where he then was, on a pilgrimage to Saint James of Compostela. After this they rose from the table, said grace and went into the fields to listen to the nightingales, and crossed to the islets in the Seine to watch fish being caught. They were all so enchanted by this long and happy day that it was late when at last they went to bed. Next morning they went to hear Mass in the great priory church, which stood close to the entrance to the grounds. Then they took leave of the 'ladies' but did not apparently see the Prioress or the nuns again, mounted their horses and rode off into the forest.

Up to this point Christine's poem is remarkable not only for its cheerful charm but for the ring of truth in every line. Even in the idyllic beginning one feels the actual joy of the company in their expedition, while in the detailed narrative of her account of the priory and their doings there and in Poissy itself she captures all the pleasure and interest which she obviously experienced throughout that day. But it was such a personal story that she felt it would not quite do as a poem for the Seneschal of Hainault, or rather that it was not quite enough as a subject. So she appended as a final section to her poem an account of two lovers with whom she says she talked on their homeward journey. And this, though not without interest in itself and as the first example of the amorous debate type of poem at which Christine was to excel, is clearly a literary artifice in strong contrast with the personal story in the first part of the work.

As they rode homeward, she says, she noticed that two of her youthful companions were not as happy as the rest. One of these was the most beautiful of the girls and the other a young esquire. She persuaded them to tell each other the cause of their sorrow and after some hesitation they agreed. The girl then related how for more than seven years she had loved a noble and beautiful knight whose physical charms and many qualities she described in minute detail. But five years ago he went to Turkey to take part in that battle of Nicopolis where so many of the French nobility died and where he was taken prisoner. There he had remained ever since because his family could not manage to pay his ransom. The esquire then told his less dramatic but still cruel story of how for five years he had loved a lady, whose beauty he also extols in detail, but who did not return his love. The girl thinks her case is the worse, as he can at least see his love; but he thinks himself the unhappier of the two since she knows her knight loves her whereas his lady does not love him. They begged Christine to submit their case to an impartial judge and she agreed to ask the Seneschal of Hainault to adjudicate. Whereupon they joined the rest of the party and, as they were now nearing Paris, they ended the day by dining with Christine.

When they had gone she sat down to write her poem, prefacing it with a few lines in which she does not actually name the Seneschal but is plainly addressing him. She reminded him of how he had once sent her a message when he was abroad, to say he would like a poem concerning two lovers who had asked her to find someone to judge their cases. So she has now chosen him to judge this one. To come to what interests him as soon as possible she says she will 'abridge' the story of the poem, whereupon she launches into her account of her visit to Poissy, to see 'a daughter I have, beautiful and sweet, young and well-read', and thereafter continues with the story of the visit which, fortunately, she did not after all find herself able to 'abridge'.

What the Seneschal thought of her poem of course we never hear.

But it is to be presumed that he liked it and told her so and perhaps even asked her for another. For some time later she sent him another poem, *Le Livre des Trois Jugemens*,[2] submitting three different problems of lovers to his judgment. In this Christine does not, as in the *Dit de Poissy*, paint a scene where the situation arises, but with obvious artifice pretends that the lovers in question have asked her to judge between them and that she has chosen rather to submit their stories to the Seneschal. The poem is chiefly of interest as showing the kind of moral and ethical attitudes in matters of love prevalent at the time, and the kind of questions debated at the Courts of Love.

One would like to know what the Seneschal's judgment was in these three cases, but though there is no record of it it is not at all unlikely that he gave it, for many of the greatest knights and nobles of the time enjoyed debating such questions, especially since they themselves were often involved in similar stories. On the whole, however, Jean de Werchin was more at home in feats of arms, either in genuine wars or in duels arising from some private cause, as he was to show later.* We do not know when *Le Livre des Trois Jugemens* was written, but as it is a slight and comparatively uninspired work it would seem to have been thrown off rather quickly—perhaps, as suggested, in response to a request—and certainly to have been written before the third and last of Christine's debate poems, *Le Débat de Deux Amants*[3] which, on internal evidence, can be dated 1401, the year after *Le Dit de Poissy*. This time she chose a patron not only much nearer home but more influential: Louis of Orleans. In her opening lines she begs him to listen to her little story and not to despise it, telling him that she had written it to solace him in the midst of the many cares that weigh on important persons like himself, whose qualities she praises. But as her tale is of a debate between lovers they need a judge, and both they and she beg him to undertake this task, knowing how just his judgments are.

Christine by now was obviously on good social terms with Louis, for she took as the scene of the debate in the poem a party which he gave in one of his many houses in Paris—something she would hardly have done if she had not herself been one of the guests invited to it. She does not tell us at which of his many houses it took place. One of the most important of these was the Hôtel d'Orleans, the site of which in the rue Saint André-des-Arts is still marked. Another was the Hôtel de Boheme

* See page 87 below.

near the Louvre. But in 1401 he had just taken possession of a great house which he had built on a vast site the king had given him five years before, not far from the Bastille, the Hôtel Saint Pol and the monastery of the Celestines, to which he was so devoted.[4] He had planted large gardens round it, and as much of the action of the poem takes place in the garden, it may be that Louis was inaugurating his new palace by giving one of his customary lavish entertainments there.

It took place in the month of May and Christine describes the company of gay, young and beautiful people who met in this splendid house, to enjoy themselves dancing, listening to minstrels and playing games. Christine, who says she had had no heart for such pastimes since her husband died, sat on a bench by herself, watching the company with sympathetic eyes. Most of them were light-hearted but occasionally she observed a couple 'whose hearts were becoming interlaced through the looks they were exchanging'. And there were others who were obviously already a prey to love. Beside a window to the right of where she was sitting there was a knight who, though young and well-dressed, was pale and sad, leant his head on his right hand, kept saying 'alas!' and even sometimes wept. She guessed the cause of his unhappiness because he changed colour when a certain lady passed near him. Only Christine noticed his look, it was 'so subtle'; but when he realised she had seen it, he rose and came over to her. Not wanting to upset him she began to move away, but he made her sit down again and asked her: 'What are you thinking of alone here? Why aren't you dancing?'

At that point there came up a delightful young esquire, whom she had also noticed, who sang and danced so well that it seemed that 'the world was his'. But though he was obviously enjoying himself with everybody, she had noticed that he too must be in love, because he was always looking at one lady in particular. Preoccupied as both he and the sad knight were with their feelings, they fell to talking of love so earnestly that Christine suggested they should leave the house to go and sit in the garden to talk in peace where none could hear them. In order to make their discussion more general she proposed that they should take another woman with them. So they invited a 'pleasant bourgeoise' and all repaired to the delightful garden.

After some discussion as to who should begin, the sad knight agrees to and says he thinks love destroys reason. It can make people forget honour, right and custom. It is a siren that can lull a man with its voice and kill him. He describes the torments of jealousy at great length, quoting largely from Ovid the names of legendary lovers who have suffered from love. He urges the young to flee from it, saying that none loves who does not afterwards repent of it. The young woman replies and her speech is refreshingly brisk and downright. She does not agree than men suffer so much from love — 'that is a story they frequently tell women'. They may have been like that once, but 'I think that nowadays their real pains are slight' — it is only in novels that they endure long-drawn-out suffering. Most people, she thinks, love nothing but money and an easy life. No man could bear the pangs that have been described without dying; but she has heard of no cemetery where those who died for love are buried. The young esquire then joins in. He does not agree with either of the other two. For him all pleasures, all good things, come from love, which he eloquently defends. As for jealousy, he does not understand how anyone who truly loved a woman could ever suspect her; to love is to trust. The esquire follows this touchingly sincere passage by mentioning the names not only of some legendary lovers but of modern ones too; and among these is Christine's friend the young Lord of Albret.

When all three have given their views they decide to choose as judge someone to whom they can submit their stories. Many names are suggested but they cannot agree until Christine proposes 'the powerful and nobly-born Duke of Orleans' who has all the qualities they need, and him they finally select.

Christine's handling of this poem is far more skilful and mature than that of *Le Livre des Trois Jugemens*, or of the debate in *Le Dit de Poissy*, written only the year before. There the two young lovers are more or less stock figures, with stock emotions, merely riding through a wood. But the sorrowful knight and the happy young esquire in *Le Débat de Deux Amants* are alive and individual, and Christine brings them vividly before us set against the background of the gay throng at the party. This is especially true of the knight partly because of the vivid detail in showing him sitting by a window to the right of her bench. The idea of making him attempt to turn her attention from his grief by asking her questions about herself is surprisingly modern. The characterisation shows a great advance too, both that of the ardent young esquire who cannot conceive that true love could harbour suspicion, and that of the down-to-earth young woman, whose addition to the party is an inspired touch.

Although this poem was allegedly written for Louis personally,

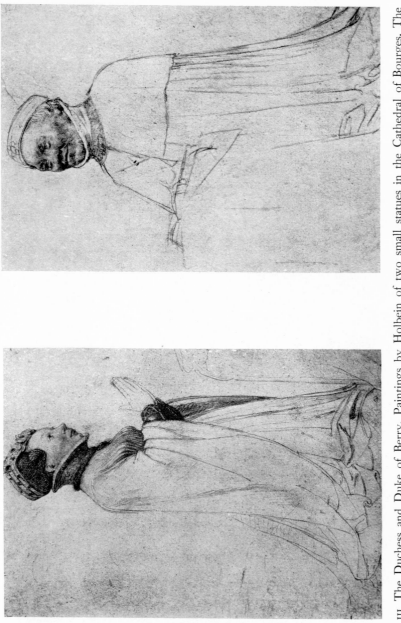

III The Duchess and Duke of Berry. Paintings by Holbein of two small statues in the Cathedral of Bourges. The Kunstmuseum, Basle.

IV The Duchess of Berry saves the life of Charles VI of France at the *Bal des Ardents*. From an illuminated manuscript of the Chronicles of Froissart, Bibliothèque Nationale. Ms. fr. 2646, fol. 176.

Photo Bulloz.

Christine saw to it that it obtained at least one other reader; for we know that she gave a copy to her friend the Lord of Albret, whose name she had cunningly introduced. The gift was made on the following New Year's Day, with a *ballade*[5] in which she hoped that he would help Louis of Orleans to adjudicate between the two lovers.

CHAPTER SIX

The Debate on the *Roman de la Rose*

AFTER her profound exploration, in her lyrics and the debate poems, of the emotions of lovers, Christine fully intended to write no more on that theme and turned her attention, with enjoyment she says, to another matter. This she tells us in the opening lines of her next work, but then goes on to say that just at that moment a young lord of her acquaintance told her the story of his own love and asked her to make a poem of it. As he was someone whom she felt she could not refuse, she agreed to his request. He asked her not to divulge his name but merely to call him the duke of true lovers. So she gave the title *Le Duc des Vrais Amants*[1] to the poem she wrote to please him. All this may of course have been merely a literary fiction, except that there must have been some reason to persuade her to write another love poem if she did not want to. And there is so much in the poem that suggests it was written to order, as it were, that one is tempted to think it was indeed based on a personal narrative.

For one thing it is so long and detailed that it gives the impression of being the outpouring of a young mind obsessed with its own affairs, which Christine faithfully reproduces to please him, rather than a work of art. The young man tells her that he was still only a child when he suddenly fell deeply in love with a married lady of royal blood whom he had seen a hundred times without feeling anything; and there is here a perceptive and moving passage describing this mystery of the sudden birth of love which, he insists, was love at its purest since he was too young to feel desire. He persuaded his parents to ask the lady to stay, which she did for the whole summer, and he describes all the events which he arranged to entertain her. One of these was a tournament, the poetic description of which conjures up an illumination in a medieval manuscript; it took place in a meadow beside a lake, and the lady 'blond as amber' presided together with the boy's mother, all the company being dressed in green one day and in white and gold the next. Another event is by contrast rather comic. On this occasion he arranged that the whole company should take a hot bath, in pavilions containing cisterns, specially set up and heated for the occasion. Yet all this time he was too timid to tell her of his love and so he suffered in silence, relieving his feelings by writing endless undelivered *ballades* which he quotes in full.

At last the lady's husband, growing suspicious, sent for her to come home again. The boy then fell into absolute despair and so pined that a cousin of his told the lady of his state. She is flattered and touched, and after a certain amount of hesitation she writes to tell him she loves him too, and arranges that he should come to spend an evening with her— merely talking—a rendezvous he blissfully accepts. This she managed at a time when her husband was away on a journey, with the help of a confidential secretary who knew how to keep a secret—a *secretaire* who could *secret taire*, says Christine in one of those homonymous rhymes she favoured. But this invaluable woman then has to go away for a time and in order that these meetings can continue the lady, calling herself 'the Duchess', writes to invite a very dear friend of hers, whom she calls 'the lady of the Tower', to come and stay with her. She dates her letter January 8th, but gives no year.

The letter that she received in reply seems so genuine that it again lends credibility to Christine's statement that she was merely the mouth-piece of the young prince. For one thing, if the letter had been the work of her own imagination, she would hardly have referred to it again, as she was to do in one of her later works.* Then although some of the sentiments in it are such as Christine would have approved, its worldly wisdom springs from an experience of life she had not had. Moreover the whole tone of the letter is that of an older woman and an aristocrat in a position to give guidance to a younger woman of her own class, some-thing that Christine, however gifted, might well have found it difficult to assume. Finally, the fact that the letter is dated January 18th and so is a quick reply, lends a kind of authenticity to it.

The writer regrets that she cannot accept the invitation, because her own daughter is very ill. But she goes on to say that she has heard rumours that something has changed her friend, making her livelier and prettier than usual. If this indicates that she is having a love-affair, she warns her against the danger of dishonouring her position and family

---

* In fact she reproduced it almost textually in *Le Trésor de la Cité des Dames* (see Chapter XIII below), preceding it by a preamble in which she says that she is doing so because it is so appropriate to her matter there. But she obligingly adds 'Anyone who wishes may leave it out, if to read it bores him or if he has seen it before.' (For this see Roy, *Oeuvres poétiques*, Vol. III, Introduction, p. xiii.)

because of it. With a note of aristocratic asperity she says that it is no excuse to say one is unhappy in one's lot. A great lady should know how to find happiness in the pleasures and duties proper to her estate. If she indulges in a love-affair she will run all sorts of risks, one of the worst being that her servants will be quick to suspect something. If she has trusted some more than others, they may boast about it and she will find herself in servitude to them, unable to dismiss them for fear of what they may reveal. She ends by begging her friend to take her advice, since her 'new behaviour has already been noticed', and asks her not to bear her a grudge for having admonished her. She signs herself 'Sebille de Monthault, Lady of the Tower', and encloses with her letter a *ballade* beginning '*Dames d'honneur, gardez vos renommées*'.

This letter so shook the lady that she sent it on to her young lover to see, saying it had made her realise so vividly how near she had come to losing her soul and her honour that they must not see each other again, although she weeps to tell him so and declares she will love him for ever. He faints on getting her letter and is as distraught as she. He will go and die overseas if she wishes; but stop loving her he cannot. However, after the exchange of a few passionate vows, her confidential secretary fortunately returned and for the next two years they contrived to see a good deal of each other. In the end he does go abroad for a considerable time but their love never changes.

Since there are so many reasons for believing that the story related in the poem is true, it is tempting to try and discover the identity of the two lovers. Unfortunately nothing is known of the one named character Sebille de Monthault who, being such a close friend of the lady, might have helped us to discover who she was. The fact that for once Christine does not date the poem affords no help either. However, there is a strong likelihood that it was written in the latter part of the year 1401, and that the lovers are the young John, Count of Clermont, son of Christine's friend Louis II, Duke of Bourbon, and her favourite Mary, the daughter of the Duke of Berry. They married in May 1400, after Mary had been widowed a second time by the death of her husband Philip of Artois in the Turkish wars. The young count was several years younger than his bride, being only eighteen to her twenty-three or four, which accords with the implied disparity of their ages in the poem.

Another matter that lends weight to this supposition is that John of Clermont was himself given to writing poetry, so that if he was indeed the hero of the poem he could easily be the author of the many *ballades* in it which he says he wrote. We know of this gift of his from a *ballade* which Christine addressed to him, asking him where he learnt the pleasures that writing gives. Was it love which taught him, to cheer his cares? 'Qui vous en a tant appris?' she asks. Christine obviously admired his looks too for another *ballade*, addressed to 'le plus bel des fleurs de liz' seems to be meant for him since it comes between that first one and a third, in which he is again named, praising him quite extravagantly and written when he has just returned from a journey in which he has gained honour. In the last verse of this there is a reference to 'her who has entwined your gentle heart in her love', and who could that be but Mary?[2]

Now that Christine had so amply fulfilled the request of the young duke of true lovers she was free to turn her attention again to that other matter she had referred to and to renew her enjoyment in it—a combative enjoyment unlike any she had tasted before. This was no less than a full-scale attack on Jean de Meun, which she had first rather timidly initiated in her poem the *Epistre au Dieu d'Amours*. What sparked it off was a discussion on bookish matters which she says she had one day in 1401 with a friend of hers, Jean de Montreuil, the Provost of Lille, who was both a man of letters and one of the leading humanists of the time. In the course of it he had extravagantly praised the *Roman de la Rose*. Christine must then have made it clear that she did not share his view and that neither did their common friend Jean Gerson, who was both Chancellor of the University of Paris and a Canon of Notre Dame, a man of the utmost probity and reforming zeal whose political wisdom and courage made him a great power in the state. For a few days later de Montreuil sent her a copy of a letter he had written to a friend who is thought to be Gerson, although he does not name him, to try and persuade him to change his mind. Although it was not addressed to her, Christine felt so strongly about the whole matter that she could not help answering what she called his 'little treatise', and by so doing she became a main protagonist in one of the most famous literary quarrels of the Middle Ages, known now as the Debate on the *Roman de la Rose*.[3]

Jean de Montreuil's letter is now unfortunately lost, but to judge from the length of Christine's reply, it could not have been so very little. She dealt at length and in order with all his arguments, some of them on minor matters; but her main charge against de Meun was still his cynical view of women. Christine in reply says again she knows there are women who deserve to be called bad, but why blame all women because of them? There are more honest and good ones than bad—women who help even unloving husbands; she could name a few such among the women of her own time, not only nobles but 'lesser, valiant women'. No one need think she is defending women merely because she is one herself. But because she is, she can speak from experience.

Apart from these things Christine had a graver moral criticism to make of Jean de Meun and that was because of the opinion he openly expressed, through the mouths of two of his characters, whom he calls Genius and Nature, that marriage is an outdated and unnecessary institution. As the important thing is the continuation of the race, promiscuity between men and women is the ideal; and one of his reasons for this view is that heterosexual promiscuity will prevent sexual perversions. Christine of course, with her views of marriage as the ideal, strongly combats this. But in spite of her indignation with it, she is liberal-minded enough to end by saying that she does not blame the *Roman de la Rose* entirely. There are good things in it as well as bad. But this makes it the more dangerous since the bad is such an exhortation to vice. As human nature is inclined that way in any case, why not teach virtue as the philosophers and the doctors of the Church do? She ends by saying that she is sure Jean de Montreuil will now change his mind and will not accuse her of folly and arrogance because, being a woman, she reproves so subtle an author.

This letter of Christine's caused such a stir that word of it came to the ears of a man with the curious name of Gontier Col who had been the king's secretary for the last twenty years and was a considerable power. He knew Christine by reputation but not personally. On September 13th he wrote to tell her that he had heard from 'several notable clerks' that she had written an invective against that 'true catholic, solemn master, doctor in theology and excellent philosopher' Jean de Meun 'who knew all that the human understanding can know'. As her supporters would not let him have a copy of her work, he begged her to send him one so that he could come to de Meun's defence. He is sending her another work of de Meun's—his *Sept Articles de la Foi*—to bring back to the truth her and her satellites—for he is sure that, being a woman, she must merely have been used as a mouthpiece by others who dared not speak for themselves. But if she will not retract what she has said, in spite of his other great preoccupations he will undertake to support de Meun against whatever she writes. To underline this threatening attitude he ends by saying that he has written his letter in the presence of two of the king's councillors and another of his secretaries.

Whatever Christine may have thought of this tactless, arrogant and threatening letter, so calculated to wound her deepest susceptibility by the suggestion that, as a woman, she could only have been the tool of others, she did not reply but sent off the desired copy at once. Two days later, on September 15th, Gontier Col sent her another short missive. One supposes that he must have read her document, but it is significant that he did not attempt to carry out his threat to defend Jean de Meun against what she had written, perhaps finding that she had presented her case so well that to refute it would be a considerable task. So he contented himself by taking a more insolent attitude still. We are commanded by the Scriptures, he says, to correct our friends when they err, and if they will not accept that correction in private they must be publicly reprimanded. Then after patronizingly assuring her that he loyally loves her for her virtues and merits, he goes on to say that he has already reproved her once for the 'error and folly' that her 'overweening presumption as a passionate woman' has led her into. Following the divine commandment, out of compassion and charitable love for her, he advises her for the second time to amend her conduct and confess the error that has caused her 'so horribly' to presume to correct de Meun, even against his true and loyal disciples, the Provost of Lille, 'myself and others'. If she does he will have pity on her and will only impose a salutary penance on her. He asks her to answer this and his other letter before he takes the trouble to counter her false writings himself.

Christine sent a very spirited and courageous reply to this letter. She ironically superscribed it 'to the very noble and confident person Master Gontier Col', and contrived, while naming no names, to let him know that Gerson is on her side in this debate; and without more ado she then told him bluntly not to keep his mind closed; if he looks at the matter straight he will not condemn what she has written but will rather praise it. As to his slighting suggestion that her views are simply due to the fact that she is a woman, she would like him to know that she sees no reproach in that, remembering all the valiant, learned and virtuous women of the past. If he is disparaging her strong reasons, let him remember that a little mouse can discomfit a great lion. His threats will not make her retract; such behaviour only frightens cowards. In conclusion she repeats that, though there are good things in the *Roman de la Rose*, human nature being naturally inclined to evil, the poem can only be an exhortation to abominable morals of every kind. This she will maintain everywhere, appealing to the judgment of all people of honest life.

Christine's bold riposte appears to have stunned Gontier Col into silence, at any rate in writing, for he never sent her the detailed answer to her first letter that he had threatened and from now on he drops out of the correspondence. But it seems probable that he continued to harass her by stirring up others who shared his views, for in a *ballade*[4] written at this time Christine makes it clear that she needed all the support she could get, when she says that, just as Aristotle and Socrates were made to suffer for their opinions, so is she for having dared to criticise the *Roman de la Rose*: 'one is often beaten for speaking the truth', she says. So she sought help wherever she could find it, among others from her 'chier seigneur', her habitual name for her admired Lord of Albret, to whom she sent a *rondel*,[5] telling him of the attacks of her opponents. These, she says, have not made her change her views; and she begs him to be of her party. He would certainly have been an important ally at this time, for in 1401 he had been made Constable, and Christine had not failed to mark this by addressing a *ballade* of congratulation on that occasion to 'mon cher seigneur de France, connétable'.[6]

She also sought the support of two even more important personages. The first of these was no less than Queen Isabeau. Christine had already addressed *ballades* to her. One was simply a New Year's Day *ballade* of good wishes. Another accompanied one of her works which she presented to the queen because, she says, she knew she loved books. It must have been in the belief that she did, that on Candlemas Eve, February 2nd, 1402, Christine sent her copies of the correspondence between Jean de Montreuil, Gontier Col and herself, with a covering letter[7] saying that if the queen will deign to 'hear' them (if they had to be read aloud to her it must have been a severe test of her powers of attention), she will understand the 'diligence, desire and will' of Christine to sustain the honour and praise of woman, which many clerks and others are striving by their writings to disparage. Feeble though she herself is to stand up to such 'subtle masters', she hopes the queen will support her if she continues to write on these matters.

The second person to whom Christine sent copies of the correspondence was Guillaume de Tignonville, the Provost of Paris. In her
covering letter to him she was at pains to describe the debate as 'courteous and not acrimonious', and as far as she was concerned she was
certainly doing her best to keep it so, in spite of provocation. She
begged him to let her know his true opinion of the question so that his
wisdom may help her to continue more boldly the fight she had begun
against these strong and powerful people. She implored him not to refuse
because they are important and she is of small account, reminding him
that it belongs to his office to support the weaker party if their cause is
just.

There are no surviving replies in the documents of the debate to
either of these letters, as it is hardly to be expected there would have
been. But it is not unlikely that they achieved their purpose of securing
support for Christine. However, in May 1402 the hitherto unnamed
man, who was intellectually far and away the most powerful ally on
Christine's side, came at last into the open: Jean Gerson. The 'little
treatise' which Jean de Montreuil had sent him nearly a year earlier
had not caused him to alter his opinion of the *Roman de la Rose*, any
more than it had persuaded Christine to change hers; and he held so
strongly that the great poem was to be condemned for its influence on
morals, its rejection of matrimony and recommendation of free carnal
relations, that he wrote a very long treatise himself, half as long again
as Christine's first letter, setting forth his views. Gerson's authority as
Chancellor of the University must have made this document a powerful weapon in the fight; but as it was in Latin it may not have been as
widely effective as it would have been in the vernacular; and it is
doubtful whether Christine herself had by that time acquired enough
Latin to understand it fully.

However, someone who presumably did understand it was Gontier
Col's brother Pierre, who was a canon of Paris. He was of one mind
with his brother in the quarrel, and he now joined in the debate with a
letter even longer than Gontier's, which he said was to be a combined
reply both to Gerson and to Christine's first letter to de Montreuil,
which Gontier had never faced up to combating, as he had threatened
to do. But though Pierre's letter is long, and deals at great length with
some minor points in the debate, on the issues that preoccupied Christine and to some extent Gerson too he produced no real defence of Jean
de Meun. He spent more eloquence in abusing her, being clearly not

only as pompous and arrogant as his brother but even more prejudiced against women, and full of petty malice. He is so pleased with Gontier's insulting phrase about her 'overweening presumption' that he repeats and improves on it. 'O foolish conceit!' he says, 'O words hastily and thoughtlessly uttered by a woman's mouth, to condemn a man of such high understanding!' He inserted this boorish charge fairly early in his letter, but at the end of it he cannot restrain his malice and it is with a kind of glee that he taunts her again, mixing patronage with mocking insolence. He prays her to be content with the honour she has won for her high understanding and gift of expression, and if she has been praised for aiming as high as the towers of Notre Dame she must not try to shoot at the moon. Then putting it more coarsely, he urges her not to resemble the crow who, being praised for his song, began to sing louder than his wont and let fall his mouthful.

Christine was by now tired of the whole business. But she was not one to leave a letter unanswered, so by October 2nd, 1402 she replied, though telling Pierre at the outset that she was now otherwise occupied and had not intended to write any more on the subject. Her letter is a model of restraint in face of provocation, and reveals her vividly as the reasonable, common-sense person she was. She says she does not know why he and she are discussing these questions, since neither is gifted enough to change the other's opinion. Everyone has his own point of view on things, different people see things in different ways, he thinks Jean de Meun is wonderful and she thinks the opposite and they must leave it at that. Although she had said she would only answer his letter 'in a general way' she occasionally found herself beginning to counter some of his arguments. But she quickly pulls herself up, saying that it bores her to go into it all again 'word by word' and remarking not without humour that if her own prolixity was beginning to weary her 'What must it be like for those who read me?' Instead of labouring his sillier points she treats them as they deserve by saying they made her laugh. And in reply to one such she merely says: 'I give up'.

As for his repetition of his brother's insulting exclamations on the subject of her 'overweening presumption' and so on, she shames him by the mildness with which she asks why he should attack her so virulently when she is, after all, saying no more than Gerson, who had said: 'Would to God this rose had never been planted in the garden of Christianity!' Besides Gerson there are numbers of wise and learned doctors and many great princes of the realm who consider the poem useless and pernicious. So why does he not attack them instead of her, when she is 'nothing but a little cricket who all day long beats its wings, making a noise that is not to be compared with the loud song of the noble birds' in the branches above it. It is not honourable only to attack the weakest party.

What had clearly wounded her most was the mixture of patronising praise for her previous attainments and coarse advice to her not to open her mouth too wide like the crow in the fable. Even this called forth from her no angry retort but merely a moving denial that she had ever been guilty of such a thing. 'I hold my deeds and knowledge as a thing of no worth', she says. What she loves is study and a solitary life. In that, she says in a charming metaphor, 'I have been able to pluck humble little flowers in a delicious garden, and have never climbed the tall trees to gather their rich and beautiful fruit, being content with the flowers of which I have made delicate chaplets'. She has given these to those who wanted them and they have been surprised at her work, not for its greatness but because it was something quite new to which they were not accustomed. In conclusion she says that, no matter who may write to her again on this subject, she herself does not intend to say any more. 'What I have written is written.' And so she ends her part in the debate which she sees as 'not at all angry, begun, continued and ended as a kind of recreation with no ill feelings for anyone'. And she signs herself, on October 2nd, 1402, 'Your well-wishing lover of learning, Christine'.

This magnanimous letter elicited no equally generous reply from the self-important canon, who returned to the charge yet again after October 30th, the date on which he says he got her letter. Gerson had also replied but Pierre does not seem to have troubled or dared to answer him. To Christine he begins by saying venomously that although she had told him she had no intention of writing more on this subject, that will not hinder him from continuing to reprove her. But only a fragment of his letter now remains and we are left to wonder whether the rest of it has merely been lost now or whether perhaps his eloquence failed him and he could not keep it up in spite of his threat. It may be that he did not even send what he had written.

The only point of hers he does answer in this fragment is her question why he picked on her to attack, to which his answer was that no one had ever blamed the *Roman de la Rose* before she did. In saying this he cannot only have been referring to the documents in the debate, for he knew well that the first of these was the letter in which Jean de Montreuil came to its defence. He must therefore have been thinking of Christine's first and still slight accusations in the *Epistre au Dieu d'Amours*, one of those earlier writings for which he admits she had won great praise. He thus establishes beyond doubt that she was the initiator of this famous quarrel and that by so doing she had become not merely an elegant composer of charming poetry but a serious writer to be reckoned with.

CHAPTER SEVEN

The Order of the Rose

I T was one thing to have defended her sex against slanders, first poetically in the *Epistre au Dieu d'Amours* and then polemically in the *Roman de la Rose* letters. But Christine wanted to do something more positive for women than that and to make clear just how she felt they should be considered. Critics have sometimes called her an early feminist, but that kind of feminism which claims that women are the equal of men in every way was far from her. Her ideas on the subject were much more reasonable. At one end of the scale she resented strongly, as we know, that contempt for women which led so many writers to describe them as false and wanton, caused officials to think they could with impunity cheat and defraud them, and allowed men, chiefly of the lower classes, to treat their wives as inferior beings whom they could brutalise as they pleased—conduct that must have been widespread at the time, to judge from Christine's reference to it in her later books. At the other end she had no use for the chivalric code that put women on a pedestal, as creatures set apart to be worshipped. She merely wanted them to be treated as beings with the same human values as men, with some of the same gifts and virtues, and others of their own. Her favourite word for the attitude towards them that she wanted men in general to adopt was loyalty—a virtue much praised in the Middle Ages and to be found in many knightly devices.

But how to persuade them to adopt it? She had no power or influence apart from her pen, so the only means open to her was to write something that would inspire them to join some sort of Order whose members would embrace her idea. There were already two such in existence at the time. One, as we know, was the Order of the *Ecu Vert à la Dame Blanche*, which Marshal Boucicaut had founded in April 1399. Less than two years later, on St. Valentine's Day, 1401, a much more important company had been formed in the Hôtel d'Artois, the town house of Philip, Duke of Burgundy. This was not a chivalric order, but a court of love, founded principally to honour women and to judge amorous cases in which they had been wrongfully treated. It was a court formally constituted, the head of it being a certain Pierre de Hauteville, who was called its prince, and who had under him three *grands conservateurs*: King Charles VI; Philip, Duke of Burgundy, and Louis II, Duke of Bourbon. This we know from a recently discovered manuscript which gives not only their names but those of all the members, of which there were no less than six hundred. From this list it is clear that the court was principally a Burgundian foundation, for neither Louis of Orleans nor the Duke of Berry belonged to it. On the other hand, both Marshal Boucicaut and the Lord of Albret did.[1]

But its members were by no means all aristocrats. Poets and other writers, officials, intellectuals and scholars of all sorts and even some ecclesiastics belonged, as one of the aims of the court was to cultivate and celebrate poetry and music, and its sittings were enlivened not only by hearing cases in matters pertaining to love, but by poetry readings of all kinds. There were no women among its members so Christine did not belong, but as she had a large acquaintance among those who did she of course knew of it.[2] One surprising discovery in the list of members, in view of the part they were to play and the attitude they were to take in the debate on the *Roman de la Rose*, which began a year after the foundation of the court, is that of the names, not only of Jean de Montreuil, who launched the debate, but of his followers Gontier and Pierre Col, who so fiercely rebutted Christine's criticism of Jean de Meun. It is of course possible that it was their passionate and unreasoning admiration of Jean de Meun rather than any rooted prejudice against women that led them to act as they did. It may be too that they were ready enough to approve of the kind of women the court existed to defend, but not of one like Christine, for whose claims to education and independent views they clearly had little use. Then again they may well have joined the court simply because it was the fashionable thing to do.

But neither the Order of the *Ecu Vert à la Dame Blanche* nor the Burgundian Court of Love was exactly the kind of foundation that Christine felt would truly embody her ideal. Marshal Boucicaut's Order had after all been expressly formed to help a particular class of women, those 'ladies and maidens of noble lineage' whom powerful men had persecuted when their menfolk were fighting abroad. Christine on the other hand felt that all women, irrespective of rank, should be protected against such treatment. As for the Court of Love, apart from its cultural preoccupations, it was chiefly concerned with the chivalrous treatment of women by men in a love relationship, whereas what Christine wanted was to change the attitude of men towards women in general, instilling into them that natural respect which she called 'loyalty'. There was clearly room for yet a third association. And the name Christine dreamt of for it was the Order of the Rose, as though to rescue this flower from the besmirching it had recently suffered and make of it again a symbol of purity and perfection.

Whether in fact such an order was ever founded, or whether the poem in which Christine tells us of it was a work of pure fantasy, we cannot know. Certainly the first part of the poem seems to describe an actual gathering to that end, even though it may have been no more than an elegant charade which Louis of Orleans, knowing her ideas, organised to please her, and which she afterwards chronicled for him in the *Dit de la Rose*.[3] This poem, one of her most exquisite, is like a series of ravishingly coloured scenes, where the courtly figures pass and re-pass as in a graceful dance, and where the narrative, adorned with many delightful touches of poetic imagination, is interspersed with some of her happiest *ballades*.

The occasion she describes took place, she says, on St Valentine's day in 1402 in one of Louis' many palaces. With the exception of herself, all the guests were members of his own household, an indication of how much in his favour she was. As he did not want strangers to be present, the doors were closed when the last guest had arrived, and first they all sat down to a delicious supper, where there was not only much laughter and good cheer, but where most of the talk, as usual in courts of love, was of courtesy and honour.

Then suddenly, and magically, there appeared amongst them, in the midst of a great light, a lady whose name was Loyalty, attended by young girls carrying gilded cups. She said she brought them greetings from the God of Love, who had sent them roses on condition they swore never to speak ill of women. These she placed in the gilded cups, together with a scroll with the text of an oath, which each who took a rose must swear to keep, repeating that he would guard the honour of women

> *en toute chose*
> *Et pour ce prens l'Ordre de la Rose*

After this the company, laughing and singing, took their leave.

When they had all gone Christine seems to have felt that in this light-hearted description of an imaginary charade, she had not sufficiently driven home her serious purpose. So she continued her poem by saying that in her sleep that night the goddess Loyalty appeared to her again, bringing a special message from the God of Love to the effect that he too hated all those, of whatever walk in life, who speak ill of women. This was why he had sent Loyalty to institute the new Order. He wanted it to be known in all lands, even where roses do not grow, for they can be made of gold or silver. Only women may confer it. Before Loyalty disappeared she left with Christine an exquisite document, written in azure letters on gold parchment, setting down the rules of the Order. As the owner of it, she is empowered to make it known everywhere—a poetic way in which Christine justifies her lifelong mission of improving the status of women.

It is no good looking today in the annals of medieval heraldry for the Order of the Rose. But whether or not it ever existed or was only a figment of Christine's imagination, she certainly made of it an enchanting poem and one which might easily have had some influence on the society of her time. One feels her sensuous pleasure, as a poet and a woman, in all the colour and movements she describes in this poem that is like a brief interlude when, thankfully ending her wordy warfare on the subject of the *Roman de la Rose*, she treads once again the flowery paths of poetry before turning to the serious study that from childhood she had been longing for, and the more original and ambitious works for which it was to prepare her.

CHAPTER EIGHT

The Joy and the First Fruits of Learning

CHRISTINE had in fact been reading zealously since the beginning of 1400, or even perhaps a little earlier, as soon as the settlement of her financial affairs gave her a little leisure. There had never been any doubt in her mind that learning, the greatest of all riches, as she called it in one of her poems,[1] was the thing that mattered most to her. 'There is no lovelier occupation', she declared, 'nor one that makes people more complete.'[2] She was in any case naturally inclined to it and considered herself fortunate 'because God and nature had granted to me, beyond the common run of women, the gift of the love of learning'. She would say to children 'if you only knew what a splendid thing it is to have a liking for knowledge, and how wretched it is to be ignorant!' And when one day a man disapproved of her desire to learn, saying that it does not become a woman to be so learned, as few of them are, she retorted aptly that it less becomes a man to be ignorant, as so many of them are. But it really did not matter to her what people thought, she was filled with a passion for reading and study and every word she says about this passion reveals the excitement she felt at the thought of the discoveries that lay ahead, an excitement all the greater from having to be repressed for so long. And so, she says, she 'closed the doors of her senses to outward things, and turned to beautiful books'.

These were available to her in many places, beginning with her own home. For in her little study, where so many miniatures in her manuscripts show her sitting comfortably at her desk, with her pen and her inkwell on it, and often with her small white dog at her feet, she had the books she had inherited from her father, some of which had been given to him by Charles V. She would also certainly have been able to borrow books from such friendly officials as Guillaume de Tignonville, Bureau de la Rivière and Jean de Montagu, all of whom were bookish, as was of course much more so Jean Gerson. Through him too, she could have had access to the University library. She was hardly on sufficiently familiar terms with the Dukes of Berry and

Burgundy to borrow their books, but her patron Louis of Orleans, a great collector, would undoubtedly have allowed his protégée to make use of his library, which he was then busy building up.

Finally there was the king's library, whose librarian, Gilles Malet, was a friend of hers.[3] This was not the creation of Charles VI, but that of his illustrious father who, just at the time when Christine first came to Paris at the age of four or five, was installing it in one of the towers, called the *Tour de la Fauconnerie*, of his palace of the *Louvre*. The library at first occupied two floors of this tower, but soon overflowed into a third. The rooms were beautiful, as the walls were panelled in *'bois d'Irlande'* (bog-oak perhaps?) which had been given to the king by the Seneschal of Hainault, while the ceilings were of cypress wood. The windows were covered with some sort of metal netting to keep out the birds and 'other beasts'. There were newly made benches for the readers, as the old ones in the palace where the library had been before were too old. In addition to a silver lamp which hung from the roof, there were thirty little chandeliers which enabled readers to work at night. At the end of the reign of Charles V the library contained 900 manuscripts, but during that of his son Charles, although he made some additions to it, the books were so often borrowed and not returned by members of the royal family, in spite of the vigilance of Gilles Malet, that the collection was much diminished.

With the field wide open before her, and being methodical by nature, Christine felt the need to make some sort of reading-plan. And so, she says, like a child beginning with its A B C D, she started with histories from the beginning of the world, tackling first the Hebrews and Assyrians and coming down to the Romans, the French and the Britons. Unfortunately she does not give us the titles of the books she read, so these have to be deduced partly from our knowledge of what was available[4] and partly from her mentioning of the names of writers, chiefly ancient writers, in her own subsequent works. The likeliest book of universal history at her disposal was a very popular volume, the *Histoire ancienne jusqu'a César*. There were available individual histories too, such as that of Alexander the Great, one of the most popular stories of the Middle Ages, of which a Latin account of the eleventh century had been translated into French. When it came to France the *Grandes Chroniques de France* were a great source-book, especially as the writer followed the custom of the time by beginning the history of France in some far-off almost mythical period. Another great contemporary chronicle which we know she read was that by Le Religieux de Saint Denys.

In the minds of many people at that time actual history seems to have merged very closely with legends and mythology. The story of Troy, for instance, in the huge twelfth-century compilation of Benoît de Sainte-Maure, from which other versions such as the *Vraye Histoire de Troye* were later taken, was so familiar to all educated persons that it must have been difficult to believe that its heroes had not once existed. Similarly with the mythological characters of Ovid's *Metamorphoses* and Boccaccio's *De Genealogia Deorum*. With the goddesses especially, Christine had a tendency to think of them as real people, when for instance she says that she and Minerva were both Italians. And indeed it sometimes is difficult to be sure whether the saints and martyrs in *The Golden Legend* of Voragine or in such books as Vincent de Beauvais' *Miroir Historial*—another very popular book at the time—had actually lived or were merely imaginary embodiments of virtue.

When it came to what she calls 'the deductions of the sciences', a word by which she means specialised subjects, she obviously felt she was in deeper waters and is careful to remark that she had not the presumption to attack those she could not understand, remembering Cato who had said that 'reading without understanding is not reading'. She does not say what those subjects were, but she was probably thinking of mathematics, alchemy and astronomy rather than philosophy, theology and morals, for which she had a particular liking. Just what she knew of them, however, it is difficult to determine. She constantly refers to Aristotle's *Metaphysics*, but as it is most unlikely that she knew Greek she must have read this in some French translation, rather than a Latin one, for it is improbable that she knew much Latin either.

But even in translation she would not have had time to read the works of all the writers whose works she quotes. The one book of philosophy which we know that, like all her contemporaries, she read was the *De Consolatione Philosophiae* of Boethius. For the rest there was ready to her hand the *Dicta Philosophorum*, an anthology of the sayings of the philosophers and other ancient writers which Guillaume de Tignonville had translated. It seems equally certain that she obtained her knowledge of the Fathers, of whom she refers to Ambrose, Augustine, Gregory, Isidore, Jerome and Origen, and her knowledge of the Bible too, from the innumerable anthologies and encyclopaedias which were compiled then to be used in just that way. Christine was not pretending to more knowledge than she had in so using them. One should rather praise her for the clear head and method that enabled her to classify the knowledge so obtained and to put it to apt uses, fortifying her own observations and impressions with ancient wisdom.

If all these histories and legends fascinated her, it was the poets who aroused her greatest enthusiasm and with whom she felt the most affinity. Of them the one she admired above all others was Dante whose great poem, she had told Pierre Col, was a thousand times better composed and more subtle than the *Roman de la Rose*, adding teasingly that he would have to get someone to 'expound' it to him, since it was written in the purest Florentine. She could have read Petrarch in Italian, although rather surprisingly she does not mention him. Of the Romans, Virgil, Ovid and Horace are the poets she most praises, although it is unlikely she read them in any but French translations. She quotes no names of her own forerunners in France and only one of her contemporaries—Eustache Deschamps, of whom she had a high opinion, even though his views on marriage, in his *Le Miroir de Mariage*, by no means agreed with her own. What particularly intrigued her in the poets was partly their use of allegory and parable— what she called their 'subtle coverings' and 'beautiful matter hidden under delectable and moral fictions'—and partly their style. It took her some time before she was able to penetrate their meanings and to appreciate the full beauty of their metres and rhetoric. But as she persevered she felt that her 'understanding was becoming steeped in strange things' and that she was gradually finding the style that was natural to her.

This she was eager to acquire, for she was by no means one of those who learn merely for learning's sake. She read in order to store her mind and to stimulate her own strong creative impulse. And so anxious was she to begin a new kind of writing, based partly on her studies, that she seems to have begun work early in 1400 on the first and in many ways the most curious and interesting of her books which she called *Le Livre de la Mutacion de Fortune*. This is a tremendous poem, 23,636 lines long, and Christine opened it with that account of her own life, part factual part allegorical, from which so many of the facts already quoted have been taken. Part of her purpose in this was, it would appear, to introduce herself to a wider audience than she had reached through her love poems and the letters on the *Roman de la Rose* and partly also to explain her title by showing how Fortune, by taking from her her beloved husband, and so ending her early happy life, had made her fend for herself and so changed her against her will into a man. After this 'mutation' Fortune had never ceased to be harsh to her and indeed Christine was to be obsessed, at any rate for the next seven years, by the conviction that she was under an evil star.

But she did not see herself alone as being in the grip of Fortune. After telling the story of her own life she described the castle where the goddess dwelt with various allegorical personages who guarded the road and entrance to it. In the high keep of it there lived all the great powers of her own day and this gave Christine a wonderful opportunity for a survey of some of them that is far and away the most vivid and interesting part of the whole poem, since it is the fruit of her personal knowledge and observations. She began with the papacy and the great schism of the church, the result of which was that there were two popes, one in Rome and one in Avignon. Christine, who never seems to have had much religious feeling, gives an amusingly woman's-eye view of this quarrel, which in her description has all the elements of a caricatural drawing. She saw, she says, a very narrow seat made for one person only, but two were occupying it. 'They were not at all at their ease there but, although they were uncomfortable, the place so pleased and suited them that neither would think of . . . taking a lower seat.' She follows this with a terrible picture of the corruption of contemporary churchmen and their vices; 'and such people are the leaders of the world!' she exclaims. 'No wonder that their flocks are deformed and contorted.'

Next she turned to England and Richard II, for whom she had the greatest admiration, calling him for some reason a veritable Lancelot—one of her very rare references to the personages of the Arthurian legend. She laments that Fortune turned against him so that he was thrown into prison by his own people, though curiously she adds: 'I do not know the cause of this, for I did not pay much attention to it.' From England she turns to Italy, a country to whose affairs she did on the contrary pay much attention, because it was her own. She grieves over the strife between Guelphs and Ghibellines, which Dante so deplored. It saddens her that he and other Italian poets should 'point the finger' at the Italians. It is true that the Italians are quarrelsome and ungovernable, but having been born there she needs must love them.

But then, as though in thinking of Italy a sudden childhood memory had struck her, she thanks God that there is one lovely city there, like a 'rose among the thorns'. This is that beautiful place 'sitting in the middle of the sea', which she surprisingly says was founded by the Trojans so that they should not have to pay tribute to any landowner; as a result it became richer and richer and none could conquer it. Its people are gentle and peaceful, rich and comfortable. There are no beggars there. The citizens are great sailors and their frigates sail great distances. There are no Guelphs nor Ghibellines, all have equal rights and they are governed by the most ancient families, in which there are many wise people. And so this city 'which I do not name' she rather unnecessarily says, sits 'without burning among the flames' for all around her are the lands of princes at war. It is indeed a delightful picture of medieval Venice.

This glowing account of the citizens of her native city makes all the more startling the attack she then launches on the inhabitants of her adopted country, France. It may be a powerful and glorious country, but justice is only meted out slowly there, and its people are full of vices: drunkenness, sloth, love of gaming, envy and pride, and of course they treat women badly. What is more surprising still is that it is obviously the upper classes she is first accusing, for when she says that men excuse themselves for excessive drinking by saying they have to keep up with the company they are in, whether they want to or not,—a time-honoured excuse evidently—she calls this a 'fine gentleman's pretence'. And as an instance of the prevailing slothfulness she blames young lords who will not get up on winter mornings unless their valets have got the fire going and warmed their doublets for them. As for their treatment of women, she recently saw a man of good reputation striking a woman 'on the bridge of Paris' because she refused to do 'what is not permitted'.

It was a bold thing for her to speak thus of the class on which she so much depended and which she had never criticised before. Fearing perhaps to have offended her friends among them, she thanks God that all men are not like that and mentions one or two exceptions, one of whom, though unnamed, seems to be the young Lord of Albret, while another is Louis II of Bourbon. But although she says it is not her intention to defame the nobles, it is clear she was including them when she says she is only blaming the vices which do not become them. She sees too the seeds being sown of that debauchery that later so corrupted the French court.

But it is not the nobles alone whom she castigates. It is clear that the state of the country as a whole was beginning to preoccupy her and turn her into the moralist she later became. The subject of drunkenness in general, and not among the nobles only, was obviously weighing much on her mind at that time. Among the common people, she says, some drink all day or spend their whole week's wages on drink on Sunday. Laziness is another prevalent vice, for among village people there are many who do their work badly in order to get it done quickly, going late and leaving early. There is a great deal of swindling too in the merchant class, with one surprising exception, the horse-dealers, who are 'loyal'. If she does not mention women in all this it is because even the worst of them do not harm the state of the world, or the government. But they suffer, especially if they have husbands who, when drunk, beat them, or are jealous.

After that, there comes a curious break in the poem, when it seems to occur to her that, having said what she wants to about herself and contemporary matters, she must now make use of all the knowledge she had been so hard at work accumulating. By way of devising a framework for what she has to say she reverts to her idea of the castle of Fortune, where she ascends into the huge hall of the high donjon, through which she poetically says that the wind always blew so that it trembled slightly. And there she found the walls covered with frescoes, which she proceeds to describe.

First, she tells how she saw representations of all the different branches of learning, beginning with philosophy, theology and astronomy. After them came the sciences and mathematics, with music, and after them again ethics, economics and politics. Last came grammar, dialectic and rhetoric. Rather touchingly and naïvely she explains the usefulness of some of these branches of learning, in a way that suggests that only through her recent studies had she become aware of what such words as ethics and economics meant, and what purpose the study of them could serve in life. From this brief résumé of the branches of learning she turned rather abruptly to the story of the Creation, followed by the history of the Jews down to the fall of Jerusalem, with which she ends the fourth part of her book.

In the fifth part she begins to tackle the whole history of mankind as she had herself recently learnt it, and relates, one after the other, and rather breathlessly, the history of the Assyrians, the Persians, the Egyptians and the Greeks, with a particular account of outstanding women in those races, for it is clear that she was already beginning to develop a cult of such women of ancient times. Mixed with her historical information are mythological stories, of the Amazons for instance, of the Trojan war, of Ulysses and his wanderings. This brings her to the Romans and she concludes her account with their history from the time of Aeneas, through the Carthaginian, Spanish and Teutonic wars down to Augustus. Rather as an afterthought comes the story of Alexander, combined with a great deal of mythological matter.

Most of all this she had obviously taken from earlier histories and principally from the *Histoire ancienne jusqu'a César*, whose actual chapter headings she sometimes uses. But this borrowing was openly done, as the contemporary custom was, and Christine's object was not only to relate what she herself had recently learnt but to show how the whole history of the past as well as the present had been dominated by the whims of Fortune. In any case it was a tremendous achievement to cram all this matter into one poem, and the fact that she relates it all in verse is proof that she was not merely copying her material but had mastered it and made it her own. One can imagine the effort that it must have cost her to relate this great journey through space and time and it is perhaps not fanciful to see a sign of that when, at the end of her fourth section, when she was just beginning it with her history of the Jews, she says that a sudden fever seized her, which so troubled her mind and enfeebled her body that she could not easily find rhymes, so she begged to be excused for continuing temporarily in prose 'to hurry on my work'. (She seems to have been subject to fevers for there is a very vivid description of the symptoms of one such attack in one of her *ballades*,[5] when she is pale and breathless, shaken by a cough and everything tastes horrid.) Fortunately the present attack only lasted until she got to the destruction of Jerusalem, after which she thanks God she can continue in her original style.

By way of concluding this huge history she seems to have felt the need to return and add to those contemporary events with which she had begun it. So she fills it out by saying that she saw, drawn and painted on the walls of the donjon, some personages and scenes belonging, as she puts it, to 'about the age of the person who is writing this book'. With this she introduces Louis I of Hungary, who had once invited her father to his court, the Duke of Milan, who had invited her to his, Edward III of England, the Black Prince and, once again, Richard II. After them come John the Good of France, Charles V and Charles VI, who would doubtless have been a splendid king if Fortune, 'who understands nothing', had not smitten him with illness. This gives her the opportunity to introduce her patron Louis of Orleans 'favoured of Fortune, who held him dear so that so far he has nothing to complain of'. That 'so far', to us with hindsight, has a slightly ominous ring, seeming to contain an unconscious sense of his future, which she was to repeat later.* No such doubts afflict her concerning the dukes of Berry, Burgundy and Bourbon who, she says, are all enjoying good fortune and, if God please, will keep France from sorrow by means of their good counsel.

Christine finished this vast poem on November 18th, 1403. If she had spent the whole of the previous three and a half years on it it would have been an extraordinary achievement, yet as we already know she had written at the same time not only that curious work, the *Epistre d'Othea*, based on her first mythological studies, but six long love-poems, not to mention that large correspondence over the *Roman de la Rose*. Nor were these by any means all.

*See page 102.

85

CHAPTER NINE

Two Crowded Years

O N the contrary, Christine seems almost to have sought relief from her hours of study, and the labour of condensing her newly acquired knowledge of the world's history for her account of it in the *Mutacion de Fortune*, by using her now practised pen at the same time, throughout the years 1402 and 1403, on quite a variety of other writings, some of them in a much lighter vein.

The first of these are four *ballades*, of historic more than literary interest, because of the picture they paint of the kind of concerns on which the nobles spent their time in those still more-or-less lighthearted days before the country was split in two. And in the first three of these *ballades* we get a glimpse of the state of Anglo-French relations in south-west France that, even while comparative peace reigned between the two countries, continued to provide strained and potentially dangerous situations.

Part of the domains of Louis of Orleans were in that region, since they included the countship of Angoulême, a title which at that time he had bestowed on his eldest son Charles, the future poet. But this territory, from part of which the dauphin also took his title of Duke of Guienne, was also, very confusingly, claimed by the English king, some of whose subjects resided there. Christine gives us an instance of the kind of thing that happened in this situation when, in the biography she wrote of Charles V, she says that his good government won over to him several French barons, one of whom was the Lord of Albret (father of her friend Charles of Albret) 'who held his land from the King of England', since it was situated in Guienne, which was 'English for the time being.'[1]

Not unnaturally, because of its mixed population, there was occasionally some rivalry between them. The chronicler Juvenal des Ursins[2] relates how one day seven English nobles informed the Seneschal of Saintonge that they would like to challenge seven French knights for love of their ladies. The Seneschal passed this message to the

French court, where seven members of the court of Louis of Orleans asked leave to take up the challenge. The combat took place near Bordeaux on May 18th, 1402, but it was not quite the light-hearted affair the English had planned, for on the morning of it the leader of the French team spoke to them of the king's quarrel with the English and urged them rather to fight for that reason than for their ladies. Whether or not that caused them to fight more fiercely than they might have done in a mere joust, the leader of the English side was killed and after his death the rest of the English surrendered, leaving the French victorious.

In the first of her three *ballades*[3] on the combat Christine sang the praises of Louis himself, in the second of all the victorious knights, while the third is addressed to the ladies who were the cause of it all. They are not particularly striking poems and were perhaps written more out of loyalty than inspiration.

Then having done so much for her chief patron, she could hardly do less when the other judge of her debate poems, Jean de Werchin, Seneschal of Hainault, issued a challenge to a great number of knights in various countries. The text of the challenge, dated June 1st, 1402, quoted in full by another contemporary chronicler, Enguerrand de Monstrelet,[4] is not without interest as an example of the way in which these chivalric exploits were conducted at that time. It stated that the duels would take place in August 1402, in the presence of Louis of Orleans, who had given permission for them to be held at his vast castle of Coucy. When they were over, the seneschal said, he intended to go on a pilgrimage to St James of Compostela; but if any knight who had not been able to go to Coucy and still wished to fight him, cared to meet him on his journey either going or returning, he would arrange it. For this purpose he thoughtfully informed them of the routes he proposed to take. It is sad to relate that, after he had taken all that trouble, no one turned up at Coucy or, so far as we know, anywhere else. But at least the faithful Christine once more composed a *ballade*[5] in praise of the seneschal's courage in issuing the challenge, while tactfully refraining from any reference to its lack of outcome.

Duelling, like jousts and tournaments, was, as we know, and as these events exemplify, always a popular exercise in the Middle Ages, especially in times of comparative peace. But there seems to have been a particular outbreak of it just then; and it is worth relating one such episode, partly because it is virtually unknown and of interest in itself, and partly because it reveals so clearly the rash and impetuous character of Louis of Orleans, and his extraordinary lack of political sense, which not long afterwards made him bring France to the brink of civil war and might, by his conduct at that moment, have precipitated a greater conflict still. The only source of our information about it is the chronicler Monstrelet, who obviously had access to the documents in the case.

On August 7th, 1402, only a few months after the joust at Bordeaux, without any provocation Louis sent a letter to Henry IV of England, suggesting that he should come to France, bringing with him a hundred knights and esquires, and engage in combat with a similar number of Frenchmen whom Louis would provide.* The sole reason he gave for this suggestion was 'the desire I have to gain renown' and his view that 'idleness is the bane of lords of high birth who do not employ themselves in arms'. This missive drew a very chilly reply from Henry, who pointed out that such a combat, although not proposed in a warlike way, would be contrary to a peace treaty between their two countries that had been signed in 1395 (one of many such during the Hundred Years War, incidentally). But what chiefly incensed Henry was that Louis had not addressed him by his full titles, and he said too that none of his 'royal progenitors' had ever been challenged by 'persons of less rank than themselves'. Clearly Henry was, for obvious reasons, very touchy on the subject of his newly won regal position.

His strictures stung Louis on the raw and in his answer he unwisely said that if he had not used all Henry's titles it was because 'I do not approve of the manner whereby you have attained them'. Then, too, Henry had referred in his letter to 'the lamented Richard II'. Louis seized on this and himself referred to Richard as 'lately deceased (God knows by whose orders)'. The correspondence, which dragged on for some nine months longer, contained a few further insults on both sides. But in the end, fortunately and rather surprisingly, prudence prevailed and no harm came of it.[6]

What Christine, always so quick to fear the worst, would have feared if she had known of this strange episode, one can easily guess

* Louis' suggestion of the choice of arms throws an interesting light on the customs of the time. He proposed that they should use lances, battle-axes, swords and daggers, but not bodkins, hooks, darts, poisoned needles or razors. So presumably, even in the age of chivalry, such gangster-like weapons *were* sometimes employed.

from her reaction to Louis' next unwise act. But close though she was to him, she clearly heard nothing of this correspondence, for her next poem, written in May just after it ended, was a particularly serene one, unlike anything she had written before, in that it deals mainly with the lives of shepherds rather than with those of nobles. And if it is Louis who is the hero of it, as there is some reason to suppose, he appears in it as the typical hero of romance, with no trace of the dangerous dueller.

She called the poem *Le Dit de la Pastoure*,[7] and the chief character and speaker in it is a shepherdess, who opens the narrative with a description of the lives of shepherds. She tells in great and often technical detail of their care for their sheep in all seasons and conditions, but also of their naïve and often jocund pastimes and their simple, rustic loves. Since Christine could hardly have had any direct or personal knowledge of all these matters, it is thought probable that she took her material from some informed treatise, such as one which had been written for Charles V called *Le bon berger et le vray régime et gouvernmement des bergers et bergères*.[8] But she makes of it a charming, almost Theocritean account and in some ways it is the most interesting and appealing part of the poem, written in her favourite rhymed couplets of seven-syllabled lines.

But for Christine this was clearly merely the setting of the scene for the story she has to relate which, she says as she had done in the *Duc des Vrais Amants*, she had written at the request of someone of 'world-wide reputation', who was well able to command her, and that it describes an incident in his own life. Once again this may have been a mere literary fiction. But if not, by calling this anonymous personage Monseigneur, Christine rather slyly inclines the reader to suppose it might be Louis of Orleans, whose affairs with women would fit him for the role of the seductive aristocratic hero. But having said so much, she then discourages any search for clues by saying that anyone who looks at the story closely will see that it has another meaning than appears from the text and is in fact a parable wherein lies a concealed truth.

The story itself is the rather banal one of the seduction of a simple maiden by a noble lord. But Christine tells it with so many charming pictorial details that the whole poem springs to sparkling life. She puts it into the mouth of the shepherdess herself, an attractive girl in a green surcoat, plump and always laughing, so happy in her life that she never wanted to change it and refused all the swains who fell in love with her. But one day when she was sitting guarding her sheep in the shade near a fountain and singing, a company of richly dressed nobles on horse-back invaded the wood, making the silence resound with their voices and the sound of their harness. This so frightened her that she fell silent. But they surrounded her and led her to their lord, whom they called Monseigneur. He made her sit by him and asked her to sing. After she had sung two or three songs, it was getting late and time to milk her sheep. The lord led her out of the wood and made her laugh by calling them for her—a delightfully vivid touch. The company then took leave of her and rode off.

Thereafter the tale ran its expected course. The shepherdess had naturally fallen in love with the lord and so pined to see him again that she became quite changed. Her friend Lorete, in whom she confided, warned her that no good would come of it. But all the same she accompanied her once on her daily hopeful visits to the wood, and at last he does come again with two of his friends. He makes Lorete welcome and they all spend a happy time, laughing and singing. From then on for some time he frequently appears and the shepherdess becomes more and more enamoured. But Lorete never ceases to warn her that no good can come of a love between a shepherdess and a great lord, who must certainly also love a lady or will have to one day. This is presumably the truth concealed in the story, that people should not marry outside their own world. The shepherdess will not listen and at last it happens that for a whole year there is no sound of the lord. She is filled with despair and on this sad note the poem ends.

If Louis of Orleans was not the anonymous hero of this pastoral poem, he was very definitely named in one of three other poems of a very different kind which again Christine wrote at this time. These were three religious poems,[9] which come as a considerable surprise, for there is no religious feeling in any of her previous work. Nor in fact is there much in one of the three, *Les XV Joyes Nostre Dame*, the theme of which is simply to ask our Lady to pray for her for the sake of the fifteen joys She had on earth. The second, *Une Oroyson de Nostre Seigneur*, has much more religious feeling. In it Christine tells the story of Christ's life and particularly of his suffering and death, and in her description of the agony that the raising of the cross, after He was nailed to it, must have caused Him, there is deep and sincere feeling. After evoking Him thus, Christine prays to Him to give her wisdom 'that her mind may never become confused'—an indication perhaps of the strain that her unremitting work at that time was causing her.

The third prayer, the *Oroyson Nostre Dame*, is much more worldly and in it she returns to her preoccupation with the state of the kingdom. She prays that Our Lady will hear the cry of the good and loyal friends of the King of France and give him peace and 'true health'. Clearly this could only be a pious conventional hope, as was also her prayer that Our Lady would give the dauphin, then only six years old, wisdom to govern the people. Given that situation, Christine's prayer to the Virgin to guard the noble Duke of Orleans 'from the snares of the enemy who is always on the watch' gains in significance. Whether this refers to the enemies whom he certainly had among his fellow country-men or simply to Satan it is impossible to say. But although she also prays for Albret, 'the good Charles', it seems clear that she regards Louis as the one immediate hope for the kingdom.

It is very curious that she should not have included the name of Philip, Duke of Burgundy, among those on whom the nation could rely, the more so as she had particular reason to think of him with gratitude at that time. For after the apparent refusal of Louis of Orleans to take her son Jean into his household, Philip had accepted him and as far as we know he was living there at that time. Perhaps it was to express this gratitude that in 1403, when the young man was about seventeen or eighteen, Christine wrote a *ballade*[10] praising the duke's court and the gentle courteous men, both brave and skilled in arms, who filled it. No doubt the duke was pleased with this *ballade*; and if he noticed the omission of his name from the prayer, Christine was soon to have proof that it in no way altered his high opinion of her.

If it seemed surprising that Christine should have found time and energy to write these varied short poems while she was working on the *Mutacion de Fortune*, what is much more remarkable is that in the last six months of that period she should also have composed another major work, not as long as the *Mutacion* but in many ways more important. She called it *Le Chemin de longue estude*,[11] after the words in which Dante, in the first canto of the *Inferno*, tells Virgil of the long study with which he had read the Aeneid. It was an appropriate title, for it is obvious that the main subject of this poem, which comes at the end of it, was also the fruit of long study, or rather meditation, and one can perceive how it slowly grew out of that part of the *Mutacion* where

Christine speaks of the countries of modern Europe and the different evils from which they are suffering.

But before she comes to that, Christine treats of many other things and it is interesting to see that, while she was labouring with the earlier poem, especially all the rather laborious universal history, she was slowly maturing and developing her power of expressing herself. So the Christine whom we meet here seems a different person, far more lively and human than the author of the *Mutacion*. She begins with a long lament for her dead husband which it is difficult to believe comes from the same hand as the brief autobiographical notes with which she had prefaced the earlier poem. So fresh and moving is her telling of their mutual love and happiness that it reads as if it was all quite recent, instead of belonging to a past of thirteen years ago. She makes one understand why she should say, as she does in the last couplet of it:

> Voulentiers suis solitaire,
> Pour le deuil qu'il me faut taire,

from which she goes on naturally to describe how one day—it was on October 5th she remembered—she was alone in her study trying to find a book or two to comfort her, when there came into her hands the *De Consolatione* of Boethius. She had read it before but never derived the same consolation as she did now from reading of his far greater sufferings. She was so absorbed that it was past midnight when she went to bed.

Even there sad thoughts pursued her and she fell asleep thinking of all the miseries of the world—wars, afflictions, treasons, and the lust for conquest everywhere. She is rescued from this state of mind by the usual dream figure, who appears at her bedside, tells her she is the Cumaean Sybil (though she rather oddly calls herself Amalthea), says she knows that Christine is worried by the state of this world and, if she likes, she will show her where its evils come from and where a better one is to be found. Christine accepts gladly and saying 'You go in front! I'll come behind', gets up quickly and dresses. Here again she enlivens this stock allegorical framework by some delightfully feminine personal touches. She says she put on a simple gown for the journey, shortening it in front with a belt so as to be able to walk as briskly as possible. She also wore a veil over her head-dress because she thought that, as it was October, the wind might be more trying for the eyes than the sun.

This turned out to be an unnecessary precaution because, in the first place to which the Sybil took her it was the month of May!

The first part of the journey went by the road of long study and one has the impression that, just as in the *Mutacion*, Christine was displaying the historical knowledge she had learned; here it is the turn of geography. They went first to Greece, where on Parnassus and Helicon they saw the nine muses bathing in the fountain of wisdom. This of course reminds Christine of all the classical authors and mythological characters she has read about, and of her father who knew them all well. Then on via Constantinople and Jerusalem and the ancient classical lands to Egypt, and thence by way of Ethiopia and Arabia to the Far East where—another vivid human touch—she refrained from buying any silks and spices, though she saw plenty.

After this world tour the Sybil, whom Christine thereafter calls Sebilla, takes her up into the firmament, which gives her another chance to enliven her allegory with some amusing practical details. The Sybil has to obtain permission to take Christine up there, which, being given, a folding ladder called Speculation is let down for her—a neat way by which she indicated that much of what she saw there was guesswork for her. Christine cannot help feeling that it looks too fragile to take her weight and tells the Sybil so 'for I had not learnt to be silent before my guide when some doubt assailed me'. But the Sybil reassures her and up they go. Looking down they see the earth as round and small as a ball below them and this frightens Christine, who says 'I felt myself being baked by the great heat' so that her heart was failing. 'For God's sake let us go down', she begs the Sybil, who merely replies that she won't melt and she must trust her. The Sybil then shows her the wonders of the firmament: the planets, the fixed and movable stars, eclipses of the sun, the comet which had appeared in 1401 and so on. All this is rather beyond Christine. She tries hard to understand but cannot 'for I had not learnt the science of astrology at school'. But in a slightly lower part of the firmament she sees noble people who personify the influences of the stars, and to whose care the destiny of every man and woman born is consigned.

This brings her at last to the heart of her matter. In another part of the sky she sees the four queens who govern the world: Nobility, Wealth, Wisdom and Chivalry. She describes their appearance and sumptuous attire in great and poetical detail. Enthroned slightly above them is the queen of all: Reason. A letter is brought to her from

Earth, the 'great terrestrial mother', complaining of the human race, whose vices and cruelties stain her with their blood so that she regrets having borne them. The chief cause of their behaviour is covetousness and if Reason cannot help her she will pray God 'to take a holiday and conceive no more'. Reason summons the four queens to answer for the world's faults. They all disclaim responsibility, feeling not unnaturally that the gifts they confer and the qualities they represent are good in themselves if man's covetousness did not misuse them. Wisdom even goes so far as to say that it is the frequent absence of Reason herself that is responsible. Reason then proposes that the only way to improve the situation will be to choose one man to rule the whole world, and calls on the four queens to decide who would be best qualified.

The discussion, or rather quarrel, that then takes place between them is extremely long and too confusing to relate in detail because each queen, in proposing candidates endowed with her particular virtue or power, is constantly interrupted by the others in a very lively exchange—at one point Wisdom even calls Wealth a slut! But their talk gives Christine a splendid opportunity to air her own views through them, and sometimes she obviously feels so strongly that she forgets her allegory and speaks in her own voice, with the usual wealth of reference to ancient authors. Thus when Nobility suggests that someone of illustrious descent should be chosen, such as one of the contemporary French princes, the Duke of Anjou, Louis of Orleans or Philip of Burgundy, Christine who, in spite of her admiration of them, obviously did not think them up to the role of world governor, is bold enough to make Chivalry reply that nobility that is merely inherited and not won by valiant deeds is not enough. At the same time, when Chivalry proposes as her candidate some great warrior, Christine points out that fighting to conquer has come near to destroying the world. Speaking through Wisdom she is disgusted by the cynical and vulgar claims of Wealth. And the only queen she supports wholeheartedly is Wisdom herself, whose candidate would be such a one as the late Charles V, a learned philosopher-king whose character and qualities she then describes at length as those of the ideal good prince according to the ancient authors, whose views she quotes in considerable detail. She begs Reason to choose one such, as only the wise and prudent should govern.

But how to find him? Finally it is agreed that the choice should be put 'to the sentence of humans' in a court of notables in the world below, preferably a court of the French princes, whose renown is world-wide. As they are wondering how to submit the dispute to them, Sebilla presents Christine to Reason as the ideal messenger, since she lives in France and is 'a handmaiden of her school'. Reason is pleased with the suggestion, receives Christine with kind words and tells her she had better put in writing the request to the French court to act as judges. Christine, presumably moved by her writer's instinct, says she has already done this. Reason approves her paper and sends by her a personal message to the French princes, asking them when they have chosen between nobility, chivalry, wisdom and wealth, to let her know their decision. Sebilla then takes her back down the ladder and Christine ends her poem on a last homely note, when her mother knocks on her bedroom door, surprised to find her in bed so late, and she wakes up.

One noteworthy aspect of this remarkable poem is the contrast between the tone of its dedication and of the earlier parts of the poem when Christine is the humble pupil of Sebilla, and that of the important second part when Reason and the queens come on the scene. For there is no reason to doubt the sincere humility of the dedication to King Charles VI and after him to the 'high magnificent dukes' and all other princes of the same stock, hoping that they will not think it presumptuous of her, an unworthy woman, to address them, that they will forgive any ignorance in the work and will not despise it, for, as she says, 'from a simple person true reason may come'. In any case, she ingenuously remarks, she has related the story 'just as it happened'. And yet, when the debate between the four queens begins, Christine boldly speaks her mind through them and that mind obviously sees the French princes clearly. Finally, that Reason should choose her for the honour of bearing the message to the French court seems to indicate that Christine, because of her increasingly patriotic feelings, was gradually realising that, woman or not, she had an influential part to play in the kingdom. And not very long after she finished the poem in March 1403, six months after she began it, this belief was confirmed.

CHAPTER TEN

Christine the Historian

ON January 1st, 1404, Christine presented a manuscript of her *Mutacion de Fortune* to Philip, Duke of Burgundy, as a New Year's gift. He must not only have read it immediately but been greatly impressed by it; for shortly afterwards his treasurer Monbertaut told her that the duke wanted her to compile a treatise for him, but gave her no details so that she might hear these from his master direct. Christine accordingly went to the Louvre, where the duke was staying at that moment, and was received by two of his esquires, who took her in to the duke. She found him alone except for his son Anthony, Count of Rethel, later to become Duke of Brabant. Philip then told her that what he wanted her to write was an account of the virtues of his late brother Charles V. He did not want the usual biography, for the official chronicles provided that. It was his brother's character and merits that he wanted recorded. Christine of course accepted and he, 'very benign', 'thanked her more than she deserved'.[1]

Although she herself assumes, and perhaps indeed he told her, that it was her *Mutacion de Fortune* which had made him think of choosing her, it seems probable that it was the brief but admirable panegyric of the late king in her *Chemin de longue estude* which had given him the idea of a book devoted to the virtues of Charles V rather than the mere facts of his life. But whether that were so or not, he had the perspicacity to see that a woman's perception might be better fitted to appreciate these matters, which were sometimes revealed in comparatively small details, than that of an official writer. And so, as the only woman writer of the time, Christine was the obvious choice. Whatever it was that moved him, it was certainly an extraordinary thing at that time to entrust such a task to a woman, and to one who had hitherto been known only as a poet, a polemicist and a writer of imaginative works; but from the last two of her poems it was clear that she was also interested in questions of the day and particularly in the personalities of those involved in them. So for one reason or another the duke chose

Christine, and by so doing played a large part in the future development of her life and work.

Christine set to work at once to supplement her own distant memories of the monarch who had received her so kindly when she was first brought to Paris as a child of four or five, and in close proximity to whom she had lived for the next twelve years. For the facts of the king's life there were several chronicle sources, the two chief being the more or less official Latin chronicle by Le Religieux de Saint Denys and the *Grandes Chroniques de France*. In addition to these two there was the *Chronique Normande*, written by a Norman and largely concerned with the Anglo-French struggle up to 1372; another chiefly concerned with the deeds of du Guesclin, the great warrior who so faithfully served the king; and a document called the *Relation Latine*, written by someone who was present at the king's death. These chronicles often varied in details, as such writings tend to, but Christine was able to supplement them to some extent through oral stories.[2]

For these she relied on the personal memories and accounts of those who had known him, particularly those court officials who had been so close to him. Of these there were still living Gilles Malet, the royal librarian; Guillaume de Tignonville, the chamberlain who was also Provost of Paris; and Jean de Montagu, the Grand Master of the King's Household, all of whom as we know were friends of hers. She could also have had recourse to Philip de Mézières, who had been the favourite councillor and most intimate confidant of Charles V. He had retired on the death of the king, but then became the tutor of Charles VI, for whose guidance he wrote a treatise on the art of government, based on that practised by Charles V. No doubt Christine would have had access to this work and could also have talked with the author of it, although he was then an old man of seventy-eight living retired in the Convent of the Celestines, adjacent to the Hôtel de Saint Pol. Someone else who might have had memories of the king was Marguerite de la Rivière, the charming woman who had sent her gold chaplet to redeem the old knight imprisoned for debt. As the widow of Bureau de la Rivière, the chamberlain in whose arms the king had died, she must have heard much of him from her husband. And finally, of course, there were Christine's own memories of the things her father had told her of the king.

With all the material thus obtained, Christine planned the work that she called *Le Livre des fais et bonnes meurs du sage roy Charles V*. It was to be the first of her works written entirely in prose, as befitting the dignity of the subject. Since the *bonnes meurs* rather than the *fais* were to be her dominant theme, she hit upon the device of devoting each of the three sections into which she decided to divide the work to one of the king's chief attributes as she saw them. The first of these she called *noblesse de courage*, which may be translated as nobility of heart, since in the Middle Ages *courage* and *coeur* were practically synonymous. The other two were *chevalerie* and *sagesse*. As these virtues tend to overlap it proved in the event not always easy to divide her matter under the different heads, with the result that there is occasional repetition; but on the whole one can discern the distinction that she made between them. And such historical facts as she relates she grouped under the attribute most appropriate to them with little regard for chronology, since that was to be found in the official chronicles. Any fact that bore no relation to one of the king's virtues she either ignored or treated as summarily as possible.

Thus at the opening of her section on his nobility of heart, after giving an erroneous date for his birth, she says she will pass over his childhood quickly, because things written about this period of life in the case of great men are nearly always apocryphal and not to be believed. All she will say is that he then learnt Latin and grammar. She refrains also from repeating anything he is reputed to have said or done in adolescence because young people 'abound in wilful opinions opposed to those of their maturity'. After this refreshing absence of any attempt to make a saintly child of him, she comes to the noble qualities of his manhood and lists these with obvious sincerity. Two of the first she mentions are charity and clemency, in proof of which she quotes how once, when the princes said he had pardoned a sinner too lightly and this might encourage him to sin again, the king replied 'If it be a vice to pardon too lightly I had rather be weak in this than too strict'. An interesting instance that she gives of his liberality of mind is that he was a rare example of a sovereign who treated the Jews with the same justice as all his other subjects. She could not refrain from referring here too, because it gave her the opportunity to speak of her father, to the king's habit of seeking out the most learned men everywhere, irrespective of their rank, and surrounding himself with them. She praises his piety, charity, sobriety and humility and says that, in spite of his poor health, which showed in his very thin body and pale face—a face she obviously remembered vividly—he was most abstemious and fasted one day in every week.

Yet he was far from being a mere ascetic, as the ordering of his worldly life showed. Christine relates the details of this under her section on his nobility of heart, seeing that quality in his wide appreciation of both the responsibilities and duties that his royal position laid on him and the private claims of those nearest to him. Thus he apportioned his time very strictly, giving fixed hours every day, first to all the business of government (including the prudent control of the royal revenues), the public reception of ambassadors and great visitors from abroad and so on, after which he always took an hour's rest, followed for relaxation by games with some of his intimates. Then came the turn of the queen and his family, with whom he enjoyed the garden in summer, and in winter listened to stories read to them indoors. He took only a light supper, after which he spent some time in conversation with the knights and barons of his household, before retiring early to bed.

But though simplicity was basically the keynote of his life, there was something noble too in the combination of it with his love of magnificence when occasion demanded. For instance he always dressed sumptuously for those great cavalcades through the town when the people could see him as he rode out with his splendidly attired courtiers to one or other of his country castles. He liked the queen to be gorgeously attired too and was always giving her things he thought she would like. He enjoyed spending lavishly on fine books and luxurious objects. Yet with all that he remained austere and his intimates knew that he intended, if he lived long enough for the dauphin to be crowned, to hand over the realm to him and himself to become a priest.

One can feel the pleasure that Christine took in thus recalling the king to whom she and her family had owed so much. And one can hardly doubt that Philip too, had he had the chance to read it, would have enjoyed her lively picture of his brother and his court as he had known them in the time of his youth. But although Christine had written this first part of her book with her accustomed speed, on her mettle perhaps to know if it would satisfy the great lord who had entrusted her with the task, she was not to have that satisfaction. For Philip died on April 27th, 1404, the day before it was finished. His death, which there seems to have been no reason to expect, coming so soon after her interview with him, cannot but have been a great shock to Christine. Her political sense, too, which had latterly become much more acute, immediately saw how it would affect the whole nation; and in a noble and moving *ballade*[3] she urged everyone, both great and small, to bewail their loss. '*Plourez, Francoys*' she begins, in what sounds like a despairing cry; and the repetition of that word *plourez*, with which she calls on one after another of those most closely concerned—the king, the queen and the princes—rings like a knell throughout the poem. Of special significance is her mention of the Duke of Orleans, to whom Burgundy's loss must matter 'for by his good sense many a fault was covered'. And she infers much kindliness in Philip when she tells the fourteen-year-old Duke of Brittany to weep too, 'for I am certain', she says, 'you would have had need of him in your youthful days'. And at the end of the poem her thoughts go out again not only to the 'common people' of France, but to all the Flemish, who have lost their noble lord. One and all, she says, in the final line of each stanza, will often repeat grievingly, 'Could we but turn to the good Duke of Burgundy!'

Philip, we know, had not been entirely the devout and single-minded regent that this *ballade* suggests, for it was personal ambition that had led him in the first place to get rid of those able ministers of his nephew, the so-called Marmousets, in order to seize power for himself. And there is no doubt that the enriching and extending of his Duchy of Burgundy, when necessary at the expense of France, was always his prime concern. But for all that, he had been the most steadying influence in the government of France ever since the onset of the king's madness, and Christine was justified in saying that his 'good sense, counsel and comfort' had been of such help to the state that their removal had left it 'full of shadows in the bright days of May'. That vivid phrase occurs, not in the *ballade* but in the prologue to the second part of her book which, after this sad interruption, she took up again. But she was clearly so full of her sense of the duke's loss to the state, and perhaps of foreboding because of it, that before she resumed her theme she had to speak of it again, and to dwell for a moment on what his death meant to her personally. It had, she said, left her feeling like a widowed orphan, bereft of one who had always been a comforter and helper of what she called 'the little widowed group of my family', meaning presumably her mother and herself. And perhaps she wondered whether her son Jean's position at his court would be affected by his patron's death.

After paying this personal tribute to Burgundy Christine turned to the second of the late king's attributes, which she termed *chevalerie*. This comprised not only what she calls the 'graces' proper to a knight which, according to her, were 'good fortune, sense, perseverance and strength', but his qualities as the head of the whole chivalry of France which made him the defender of the realm. And since he possessed these qualities of leadership and decision, the king, though no warrior himself, was, she felt, more worthy to be called a 'true soldier' than anyone else of his time. It was true that Charles V never went to war himself—perhaps because of his poor health and a permanently swollen hand; but this was not for any lack of courage; it was because he had the sense to see that, having a great soldier like Bertrand du Guesclin at his command, with an army of brave knights and men-at-arms under him, it was better to leave the actual campaigning to him. After this introduction Christine, relying on her chronicle sources, launched into a brisk historical narrative of the achievements of the king during the early part of his reign. She related, for instance, how he rid the realm of the great companies of lawless soldiers who roamed the country and were a menace to the people, and how his good government brought over to him some previously hostile lords like the Lord of Albret.*

But however well she wrote of these things, mere narration of events was not what she enjoyed nor, as she knew, what was most wanted of her. And so, returning more directly to her theme of *chevalerie*, as it was natural to her, in thinking of the king, to think also of his family as possessing the same chivalric virtues, she then indulged in some of her customary praises of the royal dukes. Her enthusiasm for women led her also to include, in her adulation of the princes, Berry's daughter Mary, now Countess of Clermont, his wife Jane and Valentina, the Duchess of Orleans.

More interesting than any of this is what she says of the two surviving sons of Charles V, particularly Charles VI, whom she describes as 'sovereignly beautiful in face and body, and taller than most men'. There is genuine personal experience behind her description of how the people flock to see him during his lucid intervals—which she tactfully calls his convalescence—and weep with compassion for his infirmity. But the prince to whom she devoted the longest and most

* See page 86 above.

flattering praise is his brother Louis of Orleans, whose court is now, she says, the centre of French chivalry. Her mention of him here reminds her of the way he received her when she went to make a request of him some years before, and it is here that she describes the impression he then made on her in a passage already mentioned.* She ends it by saying 'if he lives into old age he will be a prince of great excellence who will do great deeds'. 'If he lives into old age'—did some instinctive doubt warn her that her prophecy would never be fulfilled? Did she perhaps feel after all this that she might be thought to be confining her praises too much to the ruling classes? However this may be, she suddenly, and rather surprisingly, wrote a few very sincere-sounding lines about Jean de Montagu, the Grand Master of the King's Household, 'the father of the poor and the helper of the needy, a wise and discreet man, generous in every way, a true friend, as I and many others have found'. Although she names no one else she goes on to say that not for a hundred years has France been so rich, not only in noble chivalry, but in 'clerks, burgesses, workmen and common people'. Many sins are certainly committed there, but they are generally due to human frailty rather than perversity and cruelty; and although many people think things will go badly in the country because of them, she believes that God will protect the king and country.

Yet still she seems to have felt uncertain how what she had said about 'the royals' (as they were called even at that time) would be received; and so at this stage she apparently submitted her manuscript to the judgment of other people. Who they were she does not tell us; but they were frank and outspoken and Christine's answers to their criticisms are of considerable interest as revealing the independence of her mind and her down-to-earth common sense. In reply to the accusation that she had flattered the present king and nobles in order to obtain their good graces—an absurd charge since she had these already—she denied that she had had any such motive, stating plainly that, since she had undertaken to write a panegyric of the late king, she had thought it pertinent to her theme to write also of his 'very excellent and noble family'. What she had said of them and the king was very largely what she had been told by those who knew them better than she did. She went so far as to say she thought her praises had not been adequate, partly because she had not been told of all their good deeds;

* See pages 49, 50 above.

and this gave her the chance to remark that some people would not tell her what they knew because they thought it not proper 'for the limited power of the woman that I am' to record matters concerning such important people!

Another reproach was that in speaking of the nobles she had referred only to their virtues and not to the vices that all men have. To that she retorted that it was hardly for her to reprove princes in public; they should be corrected in private. Her critics then said that no man should be praised until after his death, when a balanced judgment of his good and bad qualities could be made. To that she replied that not to speak well of anyone during his lifetime might seem like envy, and would be repressing good examples; and she added bluntly that if she were to keep silent until her subjects were dead, perhaps by then old age, illness or even her own death might deprive her of the power of writing of them at all! Moreover to praise as she has done could not be called flattery, since flattery means false praise and hers was sincere.

The next criticism came from some who knew all about chivalry and wondered why anyone should have bothered to tell them of it. To that she answered that she was not writing for them but for the ignorant; and she sensibly remarked that it is often useful to have things written down, even for those who already know them. It is, incidentally, difficult to understand what could have elicited this reproach; for after all, her remarks on chivalry had been very general and she had not attempted to give any information about its complicated rules. As for those who said it was 'presumption for an ignorant woman to expatiate on so high a matter as chivalry', she gently reminded them of Hugues de Saint Victor, who said that wise men were always ready to learn, and if a child showed them anything they would consider the doctrine and not the person. A last criticism was that her book was not original because she was merely using information with which others had supplied her. To this she gave the ingenious answer that architects and masons do not make the stones and other material they use for their buildings, nor do embroiderers make their silk and gold. What counts is the imagination that enables the artist to use the materials, just as she has tried to use hers for her purpose.

Whatever her critics may have thought of her arguments, she emboldened herself by them to go on as before. So she resumed her story and ended this section of her book with an account of the deeds of the constable, Bertrand du Guesclin, and his knights, who were successful in recovering Brittany and Guienne because they had the chivalric virtues necessary for war which she lists as 'sense and judgment, nobility of heart, desire for honour and fear of dishonour' — qualities, she says, more commonly found in the nobles than in the people (of whom she never had any great opinion). She ends the section with renewed praise of the late Duke Philip and concludes that, since all these things were done under the guidance of Charles V, the virtues of chivalry were indeed his. Perhaps because of these discussions with her critics Christine took a little longer over this section and it was only finished on September 20th, 1404.

Sagesse, the theme of her last section, comprised in her view not merely wisdom and prudence, but understanding, learning and art. Because Charles V possessed all these qualities he ought, she says, to be known as Charles the Wise—an interesting remark since it implies that it was Christine who first suggested this sobriquet by which the king has subsequently been known. In proof of his learning she speaks of his knowledge of philosophy, on which subject he could be even more eloquent than the specialists he had gathered about him. He knew the seven liberal arts, and Latin, and had translations made from it for the benefit of those who did not. He called the University of Paris his 'very beloved daughter' and often sent for the rector with his masters and clerks to hear their doctrine and learn of them. Of his quick mind Christine gives two typical instances, one being that when he was told that some man had been wrongly beheaded, he said that if it were so it would be better for his soul than if it had been done rightly! And when someone remarked that it was a beautiful virtue to know how to speak well the king replied that it was 'an equally beautiful one to know when to keep silent'.

But he was not only an intellectual and a lover of every kind of art, he was also a very practical monarch and Christine gives one or two unusual instances of his wise and prudent government. One of the most enlightened of these was that he summoned to his council the burgesses of his chief towns and even some of the common people, to show his confidence in them; and he often followed their advice (a practice of which Christine later was strongly to disapprove). The other example she quotes, of his constant care for the well-being of the people, is a very modern-sounding piece of planning. He realised that food was much dearer in Paris than in the country, partly because so many people flocked there (even then) and partly because of the cost of transporting it there by road. As the lands of the Loire were some of the most fertile and consequently food was cheap there, the king planned to join the Loire to the Seine so that it could be transported by water, an operation which it was estimated would cost a hundred million francs, a sum which he thought not outrageous in comparison with its usefulness. But his death prevented the plan from being carried out.

For Charles V died at the early age of forty-four, before he had time to realise his intention of abdicating in favour of the dauphin. He seems to have had a premonition that he would not live long, for in 1368 when he was only thirty-one and the dauphin was born, he issued an *ordonnance* which laid down that in future the heir to the throne could be crowned at the age of fourteen.[4] As she drew near to the time of his death Christine seems to have felt that she had not given enough space to contemporary historical events outside France in his time, so she rather upset the balance of this last section by including an account of some of them, and indulging too, in a good deal of verbosity on the theme of metaphysics, and poetry in general, which have nothing to do with the king.

But when she does at last come to his death all verbiage stopped and she wrote a most moving account of it. It is probable that for it she drew on an anonymous text, called the *Relation Latine*, which only came to light a century ago, apparently written by someone who was present during the king's last hours at his favourite castle of Beauté, and who was thus able to record many of his last words.[5] Christine does not mention this document any more than she named her other sources— such was not the custom of the time. But so intense was her own feeling for the king that one feels, in reading her account, as though she too had been an eye-witness of those scenes and had heard those words. To encourage his grieving servitors, in spite of the torments of his malady, he insisted as long as he could on getting up and dressing and eating at table, comforting them as he did so, with no complaint of his pains, except that he kept calling on God and Our Lady. After a very agonising night, only a day or two before his death, he again got up and with a joyful look said to his physicians and chamberlains, 'Rejoice, my good and loyal friends, for soon I shall be out of your hands', a remark that they were not sure how to take. On the morning of his death he summoned all his barons and prelates, his council and his chancellor and asked the Bishop of Paris to bring him the crown of thorns from the Sainte Chapelle and the crown of France too. Praising the former he apostrophised the latter as both 'precious' because of the mystery of justice in it, but 'vile' because of the 'labour, anguish, torments and pains of heart, body, conscience and dangers to the soul' that it brought to those who wore it. After he had received extreme unction his weeping subjects were admitted. At the request of Bureau de la Rivière, who was like a man out of his mind with grief, the king blessed the whole company and then dismissed them saying 'Pray for me, and leave me to finish my travail in peace'. After his final agony he gave up the ghost in the arms of Bureau de la Rivière 'whom he dearly loved'.

Christine ended her book on November 10th, 1404, with a movingly simple sentence. Although she had been commanded to write it she had, she said, found it a pleasant task for two main reasons. The first was the excellence of the late king's virtues, and the second, that she had felt herself in duty bound 'because, in my infancy and youth, with my parents, I was nourished with his bread'. She had certainly fulfilled that obligation nobly with what reads like a generous labour of love written with no ulterior motive. But in doing so she earned rewards greater than she could have guessed, both in her own day and among posterity. From occasional remarks in her books we know that she hoped their fame would live after her. For almost all of them that hope was not to be fulfilled. But her *Fais et bonnes meurs du sage roy Charles V*, though occasionally criticised for not being the full and accurate chronicle of the reign that Christine never intended it to be, has been appreciated as the rare treasure it is by later historians who have drawn, although not always with acknowledgment,* on its wealth of anecdotes and instances, some of which would never have been known but for her, in this most vivid portrait of one of France's greatest kings.

Of more use to Christine in her own day was the fact that her successful accomplishment of this great task obviously did much, as we shall soon see, both to modify the current tendency to think a woman

---

* The Abbé Sallier, writing in the eighteenth century, remarks dryly that many writers used Christine's history without acknowledgment, 'as that is sometimes done with ancient sources of which one is practically certain most readers will never have heard. One hopes that learned people who do know will not take time from their own work to inform the public that such and such writers have profited from the studies of those who lived many centuries previously. And thus a merited fame is despoiled to raise an altar to one that has cost little'.6

writer must naturally be inferior, and to enhance her literary reputation in general. This book also marks a turning-point in her development as a writer; for although she was to return again to some of her former favourite themes, notably that of women, from then on she became increasingly preoccupied with the affairs of the kingdom, able as she was to see the contrast between its high prosperity at the time of her childhood and the sad decline into which it was so soon to fall.

CHAPTER ELEVEN

The Vision

ON February 10th, 1404, only a month after she had begun work on her book on Charles V, Christine did a curious thing. She wrote a letter, in the form of a long poem in her favourite rhymed couplets, to the most famous of contemporary poets, Eustache Deschamps, whom she addressed by his proper name of Eustache Morel and by his title, the bailiff of Senlis.[1] The theme of her letter was the corruption of all classes of society at that time in France, which she describes in great detail. There is greed, malice and vice, she says, among the nobles, the clergy and the common people, in cities, castles, the courts of justice and the courts of princes. She complains especially of the prevailing indulgence in voluptuous pleasures and sexual debauchery, as people no longer thought such things were wrong—a permissive society in fact. She says she knows what she is talking about, for she already had experience of the corruption of officials in the days of her early struggles, and still has. And she ends by begging Deschamps not to despise her feminine view of the situation.

It will be remembered that she had already included a short passage on the wickedness of the times in her *Mutacion de Fortune*, but then, as though fearing to give offence, had quickly reverted to more flattering remarks. In any case that short passage cannot be compared with this wholesale outburst, for whose cause one must seek. Had her researches into the virtues of the late king brought home to her more forcibly than before how much better governed the country had been in his day than in the lamentable moral state into which it had of late increasingly fallen? And did she fear that the panegyric she was about to write, not only on the king himself but on some of his relations still living, might make people think her uncritical of the vices of the great, as indeed we know they did, and blind to the present situation?

If that were so she could hardly have proclaimed publicly at that moment that she was as clear-sighted and unbiassed as anyone else. But she could at least safeguard herself by expressing her views confi-

dentially to one trustworthy person. And to whom better than
Eustace Deschamps, whom she knew well enough to call him 'dear
brother and friend', who shared her fervent admiration for Charles V
whom he had served from his youth until the king's death, and who
was well aware of the present state of things, since he had himself
written some poems deploring the laxity of the age. He was well
placed to see this for he had been a councillor at the court of Louis of
Orleans for some years and while there had written one of his most
beautiful *ballades*[2] to Louis' wife, Valentina, praising her for her
nobility and purity, her humility and compassion for the poor, in a way
that showed where his own sympathies lay and must have endeared
him to Christine, who saw her as he did.

Whatever Deschamps thought of Christine's letter, he was worldly-
wise enough not to be drawn by it into a discussion of the subject she
had raised, especially as he was by then an elderly man now retired into
the country. So in his reply[3] he did not refer to her complaints at all,
but contented himself with praising her in terms which are of great
interest as showing the high reputation she had already gained in her
adopted country, in a profession that no other woman of her time had
entered. 'Handmaid of learning', he called her and, praising her valiant
pursuit of her occupation, he signed himself her disciple and well-
wisher.

Although she may have been disappointed at his failure to express
any opinion on her views, she could not but have been gratified by his
warm praise, which might indeed be taken to convey approval of them
since he would hardly have lavished it on someone with whom he
profoundly disagreed. So it seems not impossible that his eulogy, coming
from so illustrious a fellow-writer, played some part in encouraging her
to write what is the most original and personal of all her books, on which
she embarked in 1405, as soon as she had finished her life of Charles V.
She called it *Lavision Christine*, lavision (which she writes all in one
word) because she adopted for its framework the favourite medieval
convention of a vision or dream which she says she had in sleep, when
various allegorical figures appeared and had with her those discussions
which form the subject-matter of the book. But she added her own
name to the title, as if to underline that this was no mere fantasy of
general import but a very personal account of her life and thoughts now
that she was, she said, 'more than half-way along the road of my
pilgrimage'.

The book was written in her accustomed three parts, in the first of which her aim was obviously to suggest that she had been destined from before her birth to use her gifts in the service of her adopted country, France. She begins in her usual allegorical way, by relating how one day when she felt the need of a rest 'after eating', the drowsiness of sleep came over her senses and she saw in a vision a *Dame Couronnée*, who subsequently turns out to be France. This Crowned Lady was busy making a mixture, which she poured into little moulds 'like those used in Paris to make waffles', and then put into the furnace of Chaos until they were done. Out of them came little bodies, one of which, a feminine one, turned out to be Christine herself. She grew quickly and, as she longed to see again the powerful Crowned Lady, she set out over strange lands until she came to 'the second Athens', Paris. It took her some time to learn the ways and tongue of this country but she got on so well that she met *Dame Renommée*, who asked her to write prayers and songs and the life of Charles V, whereupon the Crowned Lady, saying that God and nature had given her a love of study beyond the common run of women, bade her take parchment, ink and pen and write what she will tell her.

The Crowned Lady then gave her a very brief history of France from its mythical beginnings, remarking that although more than a thousand years had passed since she was born, Christine would be astonished that she should have remained so beautiful if she knew all she has had to suffer not only from her own people but from foreign invaders. Coming down to her own times and after referring to the good government of Charles V, she then spoke of his descendants Charles VI and Louis in an oddly fanciful way saying that he had fathered 'two little gilded butterflies' who grew into 'very noble birds of prey', one of whom had a crest on his head, like a hoopoe. Unfortunately they ignored the counsels of the Crowned Lady. Madness overcame one of them. Alas that 'such a noble bird', who might have saved the country from the evils that now rend it, including civil war, should be so afflicted! The lady France knows that the noble heart of her 'dear companion' Christine, although not born in her land, will not be ungrateful for the benefits she has received there and will weep with her 'out of true, pitiful friendship to see the days of her tribulation!'

Then asking her not to be taken in by the beauty of her face, she showed her her bruised and wounded limbs and entered into a long account of all the current vices in France in the form of an allegory in which three great ladies, Truth, Justice and Chivalry, are thrown into prison under the guardianship of a hag called Fraud, while in their stead reigns a pale, thin old lady with huge bloody nails whose name is Voluptuousness. The vices are described with a wealth of biblical instances and much lamentation, in the course of which the Crowned Lady cries: 'Oh, what a pleasure and relief it is to talk to a loyal friend and disclose to her the heaviness of one's thoughts!' She thanks Christine for her love and begs that, although she has been invited to go elsewhere—an obvious reference to those invitations from Henry IV of England and the Duke of Milan—and 'from me and mine you receive but meagre emoluments', 'your good heart will not let you forget the nourishment you received in childhood' and thus she will remain true to her and go on with her writings 'which will give ever greater pleasure to me and my children'.

Coming from Christine who, in dedicating her books, was accustomed, as we know, to speak of them in humble and even self-deprecatory terms as the work of a self-educated, feminine mind, that last sentence strikes a new note of self-confidence, even perhaps of self-importance. Had some people perhaps wondered why the task of writing the life of a great French king had been entrusted to a woman and a foreigner at that? And if so was this her reply to them, giving reasons why she had been chosen?[4] A likelier supposition is that that book had gained for her such unusual recognition and praise that she could now claim an established position. Such a position, in fact, that thenceforth, instead of writing privately to a friend she would be able to refer openly to those social evils from which the country was suffering, and which were soon to preoccupy her even more.

In the second part of the book she turned abruptly to what seems quite a different subject, but is perhaps connected with the first part in that it arose from her expressed desire to enlarge her mind, presumably to qualify for the further work that the Crowned Lady had hoped she would write. She went, she says, to the university to join the students disputing in the different faculties. Hanging over them she saw a huge shade, more like a spiritual presence than an actual form. She then noticed that it was made up of millions of smaller shades, which came and went from it, fluttering round the heads of the disputing students, and whispering in their ears.

The 'great shadowy creature' spoke to her and told her she was

Dame Opinion, the daughter of Ignorance and born of the desire for knowledge. She was surprised that Christine did not know her already and explained to her how she works. As soon as a human being is born and his mind starts feebly to work, she sends one of those smaller shades, who are her daughters, to help him develop his ideas, whether good, bad or merely foolish, as they were helping the disputing students. There is none so wise that he cannot have a false opinion and the shades do nothing to change these. For Opinion never deliberately influences people, because she herself is never certain; her task is merely to foster the views men hold. At the same time she rather confusingly says that her ultimate aim is to enable the truth to be found, with the aid of Dame Philosophy, after which she will disappear, for there is no place for her in paradise. The whole universe has been governed by her since the beginning of the world. She is responsible for all the religions. She has allowed even popes to err and the ancient philosophers to develop conflicting theories.

To give Christine a personal example of her power, she told her that it was she who had let her say in her *Mutacion de Fortune* that she blamed Dame Fortune for all the adversities she had suffered. But this belief was erroneous, for Fortune has no power of her own in such matters. This remark, as we shall soon see, was to have a profound effect on Christine's belief. Opinion told her too that she was responsible for the present discord between the French princes, since she had let each hold the opinion that he is right. 'But on the right and wrong between them I will keep silent', she says, 'for to decide is not my office, since I am always in doubt.' There is only one matter on which she suddenly speaks with complete certainty and that concerns those nobles who follow arms and think that the greatest fulfilment in life is military glory. She lays down detailed rules as to when fighting is lawful and when it is not. The sudden intrusion of this matter in the discourse of Dame Opinion is important because it is a first mention of Christine's interest in this age-old question, an unusual subject for a woman and one which she was to to treat later in a way that brought her un-expected posthumous fame.

The great shade then asked Christine if she had said enough to convince her of her power and explain who she is. Christine under-standably replied that she had found her contradictory actions rather confusing whereupon Opinion, to help her by means of another personal instance, told her that it was she who had stirred up the debate on the *Roman de la Rose*, by encouraging conflicting beliefs in the minds of the participants. This finally so convinced Christine that she asked Opinion whether she had engendered any errors in her writing, for if so she would like to emend them. Dame Opinion reassured her on this with a curious prophecy, saying 'after your death a prince full of valour and visions will come who, hearing of your volumes, will wish that you had lived in his time and will greatly desire that he might have seen you'.*

Thus not only reassured but given hope for her future as a writer even beyond what the Crowned Lady had promised, Christine ended her meeting with Dame Opinion. It had certainly been fruitful for this, the most original, imaginative, penetrating and subtle of all her allegories, surpassing in psychological maturity anything she had previously written, is enough to prove how amply Dame Opinion had helped her to achieve her professed aim of enlarging her mind. Another development now awaited her, this time of the spirit rather than the mind, and this she achieved through her meeting with a third lady, which she described in the third and last part of her *Lavision*.

On leaving the schools she went to a convent whose abbess was Philosophy. This time it was Christine who opened the interview by telling Philosophy the story of her life, apologising for the prolixity of her account, which covered not only her own development but what we know of her parents and children. This need not be repeated here, for it is from this extraordinarily vivid and detailed autobiography that a large part of the information related at appropriate times in the earlier chapters of this book has been taken. She brings this past history up to date with one statement that is rather surprising in view of the improvement in her standing and reputation. She is still, she says, having financial difficulties, because she cannot obtain the sums which the French princes give her, without a wearisome pursuit of their treasurers, and this distresses her for she needs them not for her own sake but to keep her old mother in comfort and because she has poor re-lations who depend on her. Incidentally she makes a useful statement in

---

* It is tempting to see in this curious prophecy a reference to the poet Charles of Orleans, son of Louis. In 1405, when Christine was writing this book, he was only a boy of eleven. It is unlikely that Christine had seen the child, since he was brought up in the country by his mother, the duchess Valentina. It was in fact only after Christine's death that he returned to France from imprisonment in England, and as he found some of her books in his father's library at Blois, he may well have wished he had known her.

this part of her book when she says that between 1399 and the present year, 1405, she had written 'fifteen principal volumes not counting other small ditties, which together fill about fifty quires of large format'.

In telling Philosophy all this she cannot help feeling once again, in spite of what Dame Opinion had said, that Fortune had on the whole been unkind if not cruel to her. This conviction so grew on her that she began, with a distorted vision that is almost comic, to view even historical events as having been designed expressly to thwart her. Thus it was because Fortune envied her early happiness in marriage, that she caused Charles V to die at forty-four, thus ending her father's career and prosperity, and casting the burden of his upkeep on her and her husband; while a few years later she contrived the death of Christine's husband at the early age of thirty-four. It was Fortune again who did not allow her son Jean to profit by the Earl of Salisbury's offer to bring him up in England by causing Salisbury's death; and since this was due to the deposition and death of Richard II, the implication almost is that Fortune contrived this too in order to ruin her son's future hopes. Other notable deaths brought about by Fortune were those of the Duke of Milan soon after his offer of hospitality to Christine, and finally that of Philip the Bold, coming so quickly after he had commissioned her life of Charles V.

It was no wonder that Philosophy, after hearing this catalogue of complaints, took Christine briskly to task, telling her that she is ungrateful for the good things she has received: her fine and noble parents, her splendid children, especially that daughter of hers who tries in her letters to console her mother and make her hate the world, and thirdly the fact that she had been given a pleasant, healthy body with no deformities. She is too absorbed in herself and should try to change her whole attitude and see that what she takes for the blows of Evil Fortune are really gifts of God, who knows what He is doing and Whose deeds it is not for her to question. She is like a child who does not understand the virtue of 'the little stroke of the rod that his father gives him'. As a supreme example of the way she should look at things Philosophy tells her that God did not wrong her by taking away her husband in his youth. He did this partly to try her patience and increase her virtue, but a still greater benefit resulted from it. For, if he had lived, her household duties would not have left her enough time to acquire that learning for which she was so fortunate as to have a natural taste and which she herself had said was the greatest good in the world.

Christine ended her *Lavision* by likening its three parts to three precious stones, of which this last section resembles a glowing and flawless ruby which, she says, pleases one the more every time one looks at it. The allegory here is clear, that the more she thought about Philosophy's lesson, the more she realised the truth of what she had said (and Dame Opinion had implied): that hitherto her attitude to her life had been all wrong and that she should look at it differently. She had been too ready to pity herself and feel herself persecuted. The change of heart that this lesson induced was moral rather than religious, for there is no evidence that Christine ever had more than the normal piety of the age. But a change of heart it certainly was, for she ceased from then on from her customary complaints. To have admitted it thus publicly, even through her story of the vision or dream which brought it about, was an undeniable act of courage and showed, as much as the second part of her book had done, how much she had matured now that she had reached the age of forty-two and was, she thought, more than half-way along the road of her pilgrimage.

She was in fact much more than half-way through it, and this new maturity was soon to make her an increasingly powerful figure in the state as the situation there rapidly worsened, justifying more and more the lamentation of the Crowned Lady. For while Christine was engaged in writing that highly personal book, a dangerous political crisis suddenly flared up, grave enough to be reported not only by two of the most important chroniclers of the time, Juvenal des Ursins and Monstrelet, but by Nicolas de Baye, the clerk to the *Parlement*.[5] Sudden though the disturbance was, the seeds of it had been sown over a year previously. Ever since the death of his uncle Philip of Burgundy, Louis of Orleans had feared that the new duke, Philip's son, John the Fearless, would try to inherit his father's dominant position in the government, which Louis had always felt should be his. He had every reason to suspect that such was John's intention, for the new duke was a wily schemer and one of his first deeds, four months after he had succeeded his father, was to strengthen his connection with the reigning house by obtaining the king's consent to the marriage of his daughter Margaret to the seven or eight-year-old dauphin. Louis was quick to see the hold that this gave John over the boy and he determined to counteract that influence. Unfortunately the first step that he took to that end was reckless and foolish in the extreme, the more so because he persuaded the queen to aid and abet him in it.

It took place in August 1405. Louis and the Queen had been on a mission to the Abbey of Poissy together, where Louis had instructed some of his men-at-arms to await them, and planned to go on to Melun or Chartres. On their way they sent messengers to Paris, with orders to bring the little dauphin to join them. It seems impossible that they should not have known that John the Fearless was then on his way to Paris, ostensibly to do homage to the king for his lands, and would thus certainly guess that their intention was to get the dauphin out of his hands, for the time being at any rate. When John the Fearless arrived in Paris to find the dauphin had just left, he immediately remounted and rode after him. He found him with Louis and Isabeau at Villejuif and was able to persuade the boy to return with him to Paris, where he lodged him in the Louvre in the care of the Duke of Berry, for greater security.

This event of course provided John with a splendid opportunity to pose as one who had come to restore order, good government and justice in the kingdom, and to put an end to various current corrupt practices—including the luxurious life of the princes of the blood, which was largely subsidised by the taxation of the people. Since he himself had presumably not profited by this—he was rich enough as it was—his indignation at the practice sounded so sincere that it played a part in gaining him the support of the people of Paris, which he thereafter retained for many years. Quite apart from such popular support, he had taken care to reinforce his authority by bringing with him to Paris eight hundred men-at-arms and by appointing the Duke of Berry to be captain of the city.

The effect of all this was such that the Council sent an embassy to Louis and the Queen to inform them of the dangerous division in the nation that they were causing. They by no means gave in at once, and Louis threatened to march on Paris with his men-at-arms. But John meanwhile was making that threat look empty by summoning large numbers of troops from different parts of his territories until there were no less than 20,000 horsemen lodged in and around the city, who caused such damage that on October 15th a riot broke out and it was all that Berry could do to quell it. This was enough to alarm the princes, who all went to see Louis to beg him to capitulate. This he eventually did and a council meeting was then held at which, says Juvenal des Ursins, 'many fine ordinances were passed which', he adds drily, 'did not remain in force for long'.[6]

These events had a profound and indeed a lasting effect on Christine. When she had recorded in her *Lavision* earlier that year the Crowned Lady's and Dame Opinion's lamentations over the discord between the princes, there was no particular reason at that point for regarding them as more than party quarrels which were certainly to be deplored but did not greatly affect people at large. But now she had another vision, and a sudden and shattering one it was, of France on the brink of a civil war which would drench the country in bloodshed and so weaken her that she would be an easy prey to invasion. The *Dame Couronnée* had begged for her support and referred to the power of her pen. How best could she use this, her one weapon? Since she had no political standing in the country she could hardly have intervened with either of the dukes, especially as she hardly knew Burgundy. But she had on other occasions in the past addressed the queen and so now, on October 5th while the conflict still continued, she wrote to her again, to beg her to use her influence to make peace.

This is a remarkable letter of Christine's.[7] Although she begins in her accustomed humble tone, begging the queen not to despise the *voix plourable* (weeping voice) of her 'poor servant', or to think her too ignorant and unworthy to meddle in such great matters, it is soon clear that she now saw her sovereign for what she was, and that her letter is a subtle attempt to make the queen aware of her responsibilities, her neglect of which was to a great extent the cause of the present danger- ous situation. Thus, well knowing the queen's indifference to the welfare of her people, Christine ironically tells her she realises that 'sitting on your royal throne crowned with honours' she cannot know of their miseries except by hearsay; and so she hopes the queen will not take it amiss if she lets her know that her subjects cry to her for pity, begging her to make peace between 'those two high princes, cousins by blood and naturally friends', seeming to imply that the queen was, as she should have been, above their quarrels. Then as though unable to keep up the fiction that the queen was not partisan, Christine delicately refers to the possibility that she may favour one of the parties, for which reason her heart may make her less inclined to make peace. In that case she cannot resist telling her how much nobler it is to give up a personal preference for the good of all. If the feminine virtues of pity, charity and clemency cannot be found in a great princess, as once they were in so many of Isabeau's predecessors, where can they be?

But it is not only for these subtle personal appeals to Isabeau that this letter is remarkable. Far and away the most striking of her reasons why the queen should intervene are those great prophetic passages where she describes with vivid imagination the horrors of civil war and of the enduring hatred that may be borne between the 'children of the noble blood of France', who should be its defenders. How could any good mother look on and see her children killing each other, she asks Isabeau. Secondly she evokes the terrible danger that a foreign invader, rejoicing at this state of things, will come with a great army. 'Ah God! what grief for so noble a kingdom to see all its chivalry perish!' she cries, like a sybil foreseeing Agincourt. And she goes on to grieve over the misery that will then come to the widowed mothers and their children, bereft and starving because of their losses. She ends her letter by imploring the queen once again to grant her *plourable requeste*, written on behalf of her poor subjects, all loyal Frenchmen; and she begs Isabeau to give a little of her thought and care now to heal her people's hungry longing for peace. She subscribed herself 'Your very humble and obedient creature Christine de Pizan'.

There are two manuscripts of this letter. One was presumably that which Christine sent direct to the queen on October 5th when she says she wrote it. In the other, after her signature she appended a little poem which although she does not name him, is obviously addressed to Louis of Orleans. Although she had delicately refrained from mentioning him by name in her letter to the queen, she was clearly anxious that he should approve of what she had done. So she sent him a copy with a covering poem which is so short and so moving that it must be quoted in full and in French because in translation it loses its immediacy.

> Prenez en gré, s'il vous plaist, cest escript
> De ma main fait après mie nuit une heure,
> Noble seigneur, pour qui je l'ay escript,
> > Prenez en gré.
> Quant vous plaira mieulx vous sera rescript;
> Mais n'avoye nul autre clerc a l'eure.
> > Prenez en gré, s'il v . . .

Nothing that Christine ever wrote about herself—and she wrote much as we know—evokes her more vividly than this little picture of her sitting down, an hour after midnight, to make this copy herself because she had no other clerk available at that hour, from which we may perhaps assume that this manuscript is in her own hand. And nothing could be more moving than her appeal to her beloved duke and patron to take her letter in good part, and her offer to make another copy for him if he would like it.

CHAPTER TWELVE

The City of Ladies

WHETHER or not Louis and the Queen were influenced by Christine's desperate appeal we do not know, but as peace of a sort was
patched up so soon after she wrote, it is possible that they were. Moreover, her letter, discreet from his point of view though it had been,
must have made Louis realise that Christine felt he was to blame for the
dangerous situation that had arisen, or at any rate that he had not lived
up to her idea of him. If that were so he would certainly have wished,
now that Christine was becoming an increasingly dominant influence
in the state, to regain her admiration. It is possible, too, that he was
anxious to prevent his place as her patron being taken by his political
rival John the Fearless. For Christine had of course presented John
with a manuscript of her history of Charles V that his father had
commissioned; and on February 20th, 1406, he had given her a hundred écus for that and another book of hers which he wanted, for he
found her writings and poems 'très agréables'. This gift was also made
'by way of compassion' to help her with the expenses of marrying a
poor niece of hers.[1]

Whether or not these were among the 'causes moving him' (to use
the phrase current in documents of the time describing the deeds and
wishes of princes), Louis sent for Christine to come and see him, and in
the interview which he gave her he abundantly regained the place in
her esteem which he had always had. For in the account of it which she
afterwards wrote,[2] after referring to that first interview years earlier
when he had so impressed her*, she asserted that she now had cause,
more than ever before, to certify the true opinion she had always had,
not only of his great learning but of his other virtues—a phrase to
which that 'now' gives a slightly challenging note. He made her sit
down beside him and talked to her most seriously. Many who knew
him were accustomed to think of him as a prince concerned only with

---

* See pages 49, 50 above.

worldly affairs pertaining to his rank. And yet here he was talking to her, with many quotations both in Latin and French, of the three main qualities that go to make the noble and virtuous man and enable him to lead an exemplary life.

This passage describing her interview with him occurs in the treatise which she then wrote and which she called *La Prodomye* (mod. Fr. *prudhomie*) *de l'omme*, which translates literally as the wisdom of man but may be more loosely rendered as 'what makes the virtuous man.' It is a short work of only forty pages, which has never been published, and in it Christine was at pains to praise Louis and to stress that it was all his idea. At one point in her text, as though fearing that she might be accused, as she had been in *Le Livre des fais et bonnes meurs*, of excessive flattery, she defends herself by asking would it not be a vice to keep her mouth shut on the good that she has seen and learned of his noble understanding and just judgment, when to record it provides an example of good morals in a virtuous life. And to the reproach that to praise a prince while he is alive is flattery she repeats her earlier remark that it is not flattery to speak the truth you can yourself see, and that to praise a man while he is alive is the best way to make him continue to deserve it.

Christine evidently considered this little work as so much a personal tribute to Louis that she appears to have had at most two copies of the manuscript made. As a result, for some years there has been much debate among scholars as to exactly what it was, and whether it was not perhaps the same as another book, a sort of compilation of translations of various texts which Christine had already made and which she had called *Le Livre de Prudence à l'enseignement de bien vivre*. This problem has been finally resolved by the most notable of recent Christine scholars, who discovered in the Bibliothèque Nationale a manuscript which begins *Cy commence la description et deffinition de la prodomye de l'omme selon l'oppinion de Mg. Louis Ier, duc d'Orleans, par Christine de Pisan*.[3] In it Christine herself settles the question once for all. For after the passages already quoted in which she describes her interview with the duke and his eloquent remarks, she goes on to say that these had inspired her to summarise what he had said, 'not word for word as you declared it', she tells him, suddenly dropping into direct speech, but as well as she could recollect it. 'When you were speaking', she said, 'you did not think that I was noting and remembering your words. But when I had left you and gone back to my little study I thought the matter over more clearly.' She then decided to 'add to the said words similar reflexions by divers other authors.' In other words she incorporated her description of her interview with Louis and her justification of her flattery of him in the text and glossary of her already translated *Livre de Prudence*, which she begged him to accept, saying that it was written '*au nom de vous, très noble prince, de qui la matière est née*', which was true at least as far as the inspiration for some of it went.

Although this was a very slight and not wholly original work it has been thought worth while to devote a page or two to it, partly because it reveals so vividly Christine's admiration of Louis, and partly because there exists unusual evidence of at least part of the subsequent history of Louis' manuscript. He apparently gave it to his wife Valentina, because it appears in the short list of her own personal books made after her death,[4] which followed not long after that of her husband. Nearly thirty-five years later we find it mentioned again in an inventory of the books of her son, Charles of Orleans, made probably in 1443 after his return from captivity in England. There it occurs in a short list of books headed '*à recouvrer*',[5] which indicates that they had been borrowed and not returned. Whether in fact it ever was returned and what happened to it thereafter we do not know. But it cannot be the copy now in the *Bibliothèque Nationale*,[6] for that has no illuminations whereas the copy in the Orleans library is described as being illustrated.

It must be admitted that Christine's flattery of Louis in this short text is indeed gross, and if she had been at all a susceptible woman, which she does not appear to have been, one might wonder what her true feelings for him were. But as things were it seems more likely that she wrote her panegyric in the hope she implied in the text, that he would live up to it and might thus become the saviour of the kingdom. However, with the political insight that she had now developed, she must have realised that the chance of this was slender, and that what was really wanted was not his moral leadership only but a new spirit throughout the state, a spirit based on a proper appreciation by all those in positions of authority of the virtues needed for the exercise of their various responsibilities.

Accordingly she followed up her letter to the queen with a treatise which is of importance as being the first of those works on political morality which the increasingly desperate situation in the country was thereafter to make one of her two main themes. She called it *Le Livre du Corps de Policie*, taking the title from a common concept in the

Middle Ages, whereby the 'body politic' of a nation is composed of the ruler, who is its head, the knights and nobles, who are its arms and hands, and the people, who are its legs and feet. It is a kind of blueprint for an ideal state. It is not a work of much originality, for others before her had written on this theme. And the greater part of her text consists of instances and actual quotations from a very popular work by Valerius Maximus called *Facta et Dicta Memorabilia*, which had recently been translated, with a commentary, which Christine also uses. To analyse it in detail would be tedious, for it is a long book and often repetitive. But it is interesting to see how Christine applied the popular concept of the body politic to the immediate circumstances in France. And among her choice of instances to illustrate her theme, which she hoped would amuse her readers as well as instruct them, several are valuable as revealing not only her own character but her strongly-held opinions.

Of the three parts into which her subject naturally fell, the first and longest deals with the ideal education of a prince and the qualities which this should produce in him when he became king. We know that she wrote this with the dauphin in mind,[7] for she says in a later work that she wrote the *Corps de Policie* at the time when he was a pawn between the two powerful princes, and her hope clearly was that the precepts in her present book would be in time to save him from such a situation in future and cause those responsible for him to apply them while he was still young enough—only about eight or nine—to profit by them. There is some charmingly human and wise advice on the training of a young prince in childhood. Manners are more important than learning. He must never be beaten, but the noble children educated with him may be so disciplined, so that the sight of this may teach him to correct himself. When he does well he must be praised, given some little things (*chosettes*, a favourite word with Christine) that children like, and told some funny tales. He must always be given time for play before his meals, which should not be too rich. When old enough he should be taught Latin and logic, as are the children of the Duke of Orleans, at the instance of 'the very wise, good and virtuous duchess his wife who, like one who prizes learning, takes care that her children should be versed in letters'. Apart from lessons the dauphin should early attend council meetings, to hear his councillors speak of every aspect of life in the state, including that of labourers and merchants, to learn compassion.

Thus trained in youth he must when he succeeds follow the example of his grandfather Charles V, on whose virtues she again expatiates. It is his duty to prevent the present evils in the State. Thus, he must not promote worthless people, especially in the Church, where there are at present so many licentious priests, 'right devils' (*drois dyables*) she calls them. He must pay his soldiers well to prevent them robbing the people and killing those whom they should defend. He must try and put down swearing and blasphemy, but she says she will not enlarge on that because people find it 'boring' if she does so! (She could evidently sometimes preach too much, but at least she saw it.) As for taxation, she quotes a story of the Emperor Tiberias, who said that the ruler must be like a good shepherd to his sheep, who only shears them once a year and then not so close that they bleed. He must love justice, but she will not say much on this point since she had just written on it in her *Prodomye de l'Omme*. One accomplishment, rather than a virtue, which she rather curiously insists is necessary is the power to speak well, as Charles V did. This gives her the chance to refer once again to Louis of Orleans, whose eloquence was such that even the great rhetoricians of the University of Paris marvelled at him.

Her second section, on the knights and nobles who form the arms and hands of the body politic, follows much the same lines as her account of the virtues of chivalry in *Les fais et bonnes meurs*, and lists the rather obvious qualities they should have. But when she comes to her third section and speaks of what she calls 'the universal people' who are the body's legs and feet, she is on new and interesting ground. As they have to be strong and powerful in order to sustain the burden of the whole body, the prince and the nobles should love and protect them. They in turn deserve merit for their love of and obedience to their king, whose position as their hereditary sovereign—Christine was strongly in favour of the hereditary principle—they accept as natural. But they must remain in their proper places. This leads her on to say for the first time—an opinion she later held much more fiercely—that she disapproves of government by the people, or even government by noble families and aristocratic burgesses, as in Venice.

In analysing the whole mass of the 'universal people' she divides them into three estates, rather confusingly using the same expression as was used for the division of the nation as a whole. Her three are, first the clergy and the students of the university, secondly the burgesses and merchants, and lastly the artisans and labourers. She praises the first for

PHILIPPE LE HARDY FIX DV ROY IEAN DVC DE BOGNE

v Philip the Bold, Duke of Burgundy. An anonymous portrait in the museum
at Versailles.   *Photo Giraudon.*

vi The ride to Poissy. Christine is probably the last but one of the ladies, in her blue gown. Harleian MS 4431.　　　　　*Photo British Library.*

their learning, but speaks still more highly of the burgesses, many of them of such ancient lineage, great repute and fine appearance that they are honoured as nobles. She greatly praises the merchants too, who she declares are in general so honest that their word is as good as their bond. In fact the only class of the people of whom, rather surprisingly, she speaks critically is the artisans: the masons, the carpenters and such, whose lives are immoral and who waste their substance in taverns. On the other hand she has nothing but praise for the labourers, who are the most necessary part of the state. Some people despise them, but God, who made Adam and Noah cultivate the earth, did not. This whole part of her book is so revelatory that it deserves a place in the social history of France.

The sentence with which she ends this book, 'If I have arrived at the end at which I was aiming, God be praised', seems to breathe an unwonted sigh of relief, as of one writing in haste to fulfil a pressing need. This may well be so for there is evidence that she was at the same time, and may even have been for some years past, engaged on a subject that had hitherto been closer to her heart even than her love of France, and that is the position of women. It was now three or four years since she had treated it, in her letters on the *Roman de la Rose*. But that polemic, into which she had been dragged in spite of herself, and of which she had in the end wearied, by no means left her feeling that she had said her last word on the subject. Something more was needed. So she planned what was to be one of her longest and most ambitious works, in which she would use all her accumulated reading on the matter, and which she hoped would secure for her sex that place in the scheme of human things which she so deeply felt they deserved.

As far as we know, no particular occasion, such as had inspired the letters, prompted her new work, and so she was able to treat it without that indignation which had made her an eloquent but not perhaps the best advocate of her cause in the past. On the contrary she now approached it in an almost light-hearted manner, as is evident from her first paragraph when she described how one day when she was thinking of making an anthology, she happened to pick up a book by a rather second-rate poet called Matheolus and began idly reading it. With one of those vivid personal touches of hers she says that she had hardly begun when her mother called her to supper; but going on with it next day she found that he, like so many other writers, spoke ill of women. This set her pondering once again on that old theme that had always puzzled her: why so many writers had in the past always despised and slandered women. She had often questioned many of her friends, women of all stations in life, and they agreed that this was true.

But curiously enough, this unanimity now had the effect of making her begin to doubt herself, for surely so many famous poets, and even philosophers who were right about so many matters, could not be wrong in this one. So perhaps women did deserve their slanders. But that would mean that God, in creating women, had deliberately made evil creatures. To think so was blasphemy, and yet it seemed He had. Having reached this conclusion she mocked her own train of thought by crying, with rather heavy irony, 'Alas good lorde why haddest thou not made me to be borne in to this worlde in that masculine kinde' so that 'I should not have erred in ony thinge and myght have been of so grete perfeccyon as they say men are'.*

She is rescued from this state of mind by the sudden appearance in her room of three of those allegorical personages of whom she was so fond, the first of whom, 'laughing', began to reason with her, telling her they had come to comfort her and rescue her from the ignorance that was blinding her understanding: for she was putting from her what she certainly knew in favour of the opinions of others. 'Now come agayne to thyselfe and take thy Wytte and trouble ye no more for such fantasyes. For know wel that all these evyll saynges generally of women hurteth the sayer and not the women.'

These three mysterious visitants were so alike that Christine could not tell them apart. This was not surprising for the qualities they personified tended to overlap and it is obvious that their underlying function was to enable her to divide the task they laid on her into her habitual three parts. They were sisters, they told her, and their names were Reason, Rectitude† (*Droiture*, a personage rarely found in the literature of the time) and Justice. Reason, who spoke first, told her that she had been chosen because of her love of study to correct the widespread errors concerning women. In past ages even famous women, when they were attacked, were without defence 'as a felde without hedge'. The sisters had therefore decided that Christine should

* This and all the other quotations from this book are taken from the sixteenth-century English translation of it, the 'Cyte of Ladyes', on which see the appendix, Christine and England.

† I have substituted Rectitude as being a better translation than Right witness, the word used by the English sixteenth-century translator.

with their help build an ideal city as a dwelling-place for all ladies of good repute. Christine was understandably overcome by their command but at the same time so uplifted by their choice of her that, although ignorant of the craft of building, she knew that with their help she could achieve it. And so she sets the scene for her new work.

The notion of an ideal city or building was of course a commonplace in medieval literature, both French and English. But in general the poet in his dream or imagined experience enters a building which is already there. What gives the *Cité des Dames*, which was the title she gave her new work, its special charm is that it is Christine who builds it with the help of the three ladies; and her description of the work is so vivid and sometimes comic that it has provided the illuminators of her manuscripts with subjects for delightful pictures. Reason promises her the best possible cement and a substance more durable than any marble so that the city, unlike Troy or Thebes, shall last for ever. She orders her to begin without delay to dig a great ditch for the foundations, offering to help her by carrying the earth away on her own shoulders. Realising that this is going to be an exhausting job, Christine dresses herself lightly for it. When she had completed it, Reason tells her she must now take her trowel and her plumb and begin to lay the foundation of the walls. The work goes on apace and by the end of the first part of the book the cloister or surrounding wall of the city is built and Rectitude takes over. She shows Christine the beautiful stones she had selected for the masonry of the buildings, tells her to temper her mortar and shows her how to use the rod or line, which is her personal symbol, to help her set the rows straight. By the end of the second part all the buildings—palaces, streets and places—are completed, so that all Christine has to do with the help of Justice is to add the high towers and battlements.

Christine clearly enjoyed describing the building of her ideal city, but it was after all only the setting for what she wanted to say. And this she expressed while the building went on in her conversations, chiefly with Reason and Rectitude. She began by asking Reason why it was that so many men writers have vilified women. To this Reason gave her two general answers. The first was that it all began with Eve, against whom men have always had a lasting grievance. The second and more consoling reply was that it was because men secretly realise that women are superior to them, both in their capacities and the nobility of their natures, but do not wish to acknowledge it.

This gave Christine just the opening she needed and she immediately launched into a flood of detailed questions, which the patient goddesses answered with endless stories to reassure her and prove their contentions. Although Reason stressed that women should never try to undertake the offices proper to men, for God has ordained otherwise, a great many of her tales go to prove that they are quite able to. There are many stories, for instance, of the Amazons and their warlike queens—Tomyris, Penthesilea and Hippolyta, to name only a few lest 'it turn the readers to great noyance'. Women can govern too, both their own estates or great kingdoms, when need arises through the deaths or absences of their husbands; and she quotes Zenobia of Palmyra and, coming nearer home, several French queens, among them Blanche the mother of St Louis, when he was still a child. In the matter of learning Reason convinces her that when women do manage to acquire education they can do even better than men. That is all very well, says Christine, but were they ever able to invent or discover some new thing? This question launches Reason on instances that are frankly absurd, in which she credits goddesses, and other mythological heroines more than actual human beings, with having invented practically everything that exists, from the art of agriculture to the making of musical instruments, arms and armour, and chariots and carts. Minerva, she says, not only invented the alphabet but characters 'by the which one myght put a grete tale of dyvers things in writing in the space of right few lettres'—shorthand in fact!

After all these enquiries concerning the capacities and abilities of women Christine turns to their moral qualities. Reason had assured her at the outset that women were in general gentler, more pious and charitable than men, more sober and less naturally cruel too. But these general remarks did not quite satisfy Christine, and when Rectitude became her supervisor she questioned her whether women were as a rule as unchaste, inconstant and deceitful as men so often averred. Rectitude in reply retailed many stories of faithful and devoted women, such as Lucrece, Penelope, Dido, Isabella and her pot of Basil, and so on. She spoke too of the many wives who were good counsellors of their husbands, as Portia of Caesar, who kept their secrets and cherished them in old age. The importance that Christine obviously attached to the virtues of women as the companions and helpers of their husbands is in fact a striking proof of how little an out-and-out feminist she was.

Beautifully told, often moving and even poetic as many of these stories are, especially that of Dido, so beloved a heroine of the Middle Ages, it must be admitted that there are far too many of them and that in the end they become tedious reading. Even Reason and Rectitude sometimes seem at times to tire of telling them to Christine, for they remind her that she already knows them all since she has used them in the *Mutacion de Fortune* and several of her earlier books, which they name. But one has the impression that Christine was anxious to make of this major work a compendium of all she had ever read or related in honour of women, no matter if she was repeating herself. Curiously enough, although she takes by far the greater number of her stories from Boccaccio's *De Claris Mulieribus* and Ovid's *Metamorphoses*, it never seems to occur to her that these two famous countrymen of hers had already by their works nullified her complaint that men always slandered and despised women.

After so many tales of long-dead women and some who never lived at all, it is refreshing to come across two of Christine's own time. The first was Novella of Bologna who proved how useful it was for men to educate their daughters, for she was so learned that she used to teach her father's scholars there when he was too busy to do so. She was beautiful too, and in order that her beauty might not distract them she had a little curtain made to put up in front of her while she taught them. Christine puts this story into the mouth of Rectitude but as it is a tale of Bologna it seems likely that she had heard of it in her youth from her father. Rather surprisingly, after telling her the story of Novella, Rectitude goes on to remind Christine that her father 'had not that opinion that women should not learn letters, but in so much that he saw thee inclined to learning, as thou knowest well, he had great pleasure of it'. This is so much at variance with all that Christine had said earlier of the failure to educate her in childhood that one can only suppose that middle age, and her strong tendency to praise her father in all things, had softened her memory of the true facts. For she does not attempt to contradict the goddess, but answers her 'Madame, that you say is true as Pater noster'.

The other story which she herself tells Reason is that of a woman called Anastaise,[8] one of the comparatively few creative artists she mentions. She is so expert at illuminating and making vignettes in manuscripts, Christine says, that though there are men artists of the same kind in Paris 'that ben called the souverayn workemen of the worlde, but she passeth them'. Her detailed flower designs are more exquisite than theirs, she says, adding not surprisingly that she charges more for her work than anyone else, and bringing this home to the reader by remarking that this 'I know by experience, for she hath wrought for myself dyvers things'. One would give much to know which among the many enchanting illuminations in Christine's own books were the works of Anastaise. Unfortunately it was not the custom for these gifted artists to sign their work.

Very soon after Rectitude took over from her sister Reason she began urging Christine to choose who would be the worthiest ladies to live in the palaces they were building. 'Now put the in busynes and go before and let us seek them', she says. But Christine was slow to obey because she first had more questions to ask. One of these was whether women were by nature more 'scarce'* than men. Rectitude thinks not and proves it with stories of generous Roman matrons. But then, surprisingly, for once she gives a modern instance and it is here that she tells the story of Margaret de la Rivière, a lady still living, she says, who one day in her youth redeemed an old knight from prison.† This reminder of one of her favourites, who by this deed had obviously earned a place in the city of ladies, brings Christine to ask Rectitude whether she thinks there are other great ladies of France who deserve to be harboured there. And so she leads up at last to what was obviously for her one of the most important parts of her book, if not the main aim of it. For Rectitude replies that of course there are many such, and proceeds to tell her of them. Although Christine knew it all, and had already in past works spoken warmly of many of them, this putting of their praises into the mouth of Rectitude gave her a welcome chance to speak of them again and of a few others she had never previously mentioned.

Queen Isabeau of course heads the list, as Christine could hardly have omitted her without giving offence; but all she can find to say is that there is no cruelty or evil vice in her and that she is benign to her subjects. But after her comes the fair young Jane, Duchess of Berry, 'who bore herself so wisely and chastely in the flower of her youth that all the world praised her'. Not less to be praised is Valentina the Duchess of Orleans 'of which prudent lady', says Rectitude, 'ye might tell the strong and constant courage of great love to her lord, advysed in

---

* This word for parsimonious is surprisingly still not obsolete.
† See page 32 above.

governaunce, just to every man and wise of her behaviour'. Then after a rather conventional mention of the virtues of the Duchess of Burgundy, wife of John the Fearless, whom Christine does not seem to have known well, she turns to her dear Mary of Berry, wife of Duke John of Bourbon, who is 'the pattern of every high princess of the great love of her lord, well mannered in all things, wise, and her virtues appeared like to her countenance and honourable porte'. 'This is she', Rectitude goes on, 'that thou lovest singularly among others as moche for her virtues as for the great benefit of her, stretched unto that by charity and good love thou art beholding thereto.' Three or four other great ladies are listed too and then, perhaps to avoid the imputation that she is concerned only with nobles, Rectitude ends by saying that there are not only many lesser titled women but also burgesses and wives of men of all estates who should be admitted to the city.

This opportunity to praise her favourites is so obviously the culminating point of the book that when Justice takes over to help Christine set up the towers and battlements, one has a definite sense of anticlimax when she ignores what has gone before and says it is now time to people the city. And this feeling is, rather surprisingly, increased when she proposes as her first choice of a lady to live in and govern the city no less a person than the Virgin Mary. Christine, of course, agrees and fortunately the Virgin accepts and tells Justice that She will willingly abide 'among my sisters and friends the women'. Whereupon Justice sets to work to provide suitable company for Her and selects no fewer than thirty sainted women who suffered martyrdom and whose stories she tells Christine, some at great length. Incidentally Justice remarks to Christine that though she has found so many criticisms of women in pagan authors, it is not so in holy literature and legend.

When at long last the whole company is selected Christine addresses them, telling them the city was made to be for them and all worthy women both a refuge and a defence against their enemies. But they must keep it well, not letting their new prosperity make them proud. On the contrary, the more virtuous they are the more meek they must be. Then comes a sentence very revelatory of Christine's views, when she tells them that they must not despise married women, who must be subject to their husbands, for it is not always best to be free of subjection. And so they must be humble and patient.

This injunction, together with all the foregoing examples of how well women can do when they are free of subjection, are sufficient definition of Christine's feminism. It was now more than six years since she had had her first modest idea of founding, or imagining, her Order of the Rose, whose knightly members swore to honour the women they knew. She had now come to think this was not enough. Women must have their own definite place in the scheme of things, not a place in opposition to the world of men, but of equal importance to theirs: a great and glorious city of ladies where they would be free from calumny and would dwell in perpetuity, honoured for all the qualities with which they had served mankind.

CHAPTER THIRTEEN

A Time for Silence

I t is sufficient proof of the contemporary popularity of the *Cité des Dames* that no less than twenty-seven manuscripts of it are already known,[1] and it is not impossible that still others will come to light in time. What is more, the pictorial quality of the book not only inspired some exquisite illuminations but caused it to be used as a subject for a set of six sumptuous tapestries at one time belonging to Margaret of Austria, among whose treasures they were inventoried after her death.[2] Yet curiously enough, in view of all this, this important book has never so far been published.

But Christine was not content merely to have imagined an ideal city as a refuge for that great procession of the noble, gifted and virtuous women of the past. She was after all very much a woman of her own time and place, and increasingly conscious of her duty to her adopted country and her contemporaries. In naming the outstanding princesses of her day as deserving citizenship of her city, she had not, as she had said, done so with the intention of excluding lesser women, who might be worthy of it. So she now conceived the idea of following her *Cité* with a book linked to it but of quite a different kind: a sort of guide to conduct designed to help women of all ranks who might also aspire to a place in it.

She never seems to have made up her mind which of two titles to give the new book, and so it appears in different manuscripts called either *Le Livre des Trois Vertus*, or more simply *Le Trésor de la Cité des Dames*. The former title was prompted because she claimed that the three goddesses or virtues who had helped her build her city were still guiding her in this moral treatise. The latter is the better, since it not only connects the book with its forerunner but indicates that it is a *trésor*, a word much used in medieval literature for a collection of moral instructions or maxims, like our modern use of the word treasury, for an anthology.

It may be that one of her aims in this book was to make of it a kind of pendant or companion piece to her *Corps de Policie*, that first of her moral treatises. In that she had, rather surprisingly considering her strong feelings, found no place at all for women as part of the body politic. In this new volume she repaired that omission by addressing women according to their places in the hierarchy of the state, as in the other she had addressed the male members of it, and so making of them a kind of feminine body politic. She makes this clear in the *Tables des Rubriques* which precedes her text, divided as usual into three parts, when she states that the first of these is addressed to princesses and great ladies, the second to the other women and young girls who live in their courts—presumably either as courtiers or in some domestic capacity—and the third to all other ranks of women: wives of councillors, learned men and dispensers of justice, of solid and reputable merchants, and lastly the wives of the common people. And just as she had said that the *Corps de Policie* was written with the dauphin in mind, so the *Trésor* was dedicated to his child wife, the dauphine Margaret, daughter of John the Fearless.

A selection of Christine's precepts and general remarks will give something of the flavour of the whole work, which is one of her most interesting because it is so obviously based on personal observation and individual judgment.[3] It is moreover significant as a final expression of her views of women, for here there is no talk of their ability to rival men in any field, as with so many of the heroines of her ancient tales. She now takes it for granted that, just as for her a wife must always obey her husband, all women, however able or however educated, must always play a supporting rôle suitable to those virtues of modesty, reserve and sobriety which are properly theirs. But though their rôle may be secondary to those of their husbands, it is still a definite and important one.

Thus a great lady whose husband gives her money to run his household should insist on knowing what his total revenues are (a precept obviously inspired by her own experience in youth, both with her father and her husband). She should then make a point of seeing that her household officers who dispense the money for her should present her with their accounts at regular intervals. In order to spend it wisely she should make a budget, apportioning the money as between how much she will need for household expenses in general, wages, alms and gifts for the poor and strangers, and her own clothes and jewels, though for this last she must be careful not to be too elegant or self-indulgent. Experience of this kind will help her when it happens that her lord is abroad on service for the state or at war and she has to administer his lands for him, for which purpose some knowledge of rural law will be useful. Apart from such tasks, Christine gives these great ladies some useful general advice for their health too, which court life may well have made necessary. For instance they should avoid laziness but at the same time not overdo violent exercise; riding may be good but walking is equally so.

Turning to the wives of merchants, she warns them to be content with their situation, neither trying to outdo each other in it nor aping the classes above them. That in any case is a waste of effort because 'one can always discern the merchant's wife', who can never attain that modest bearing that distinguishes true nobility. Besides, there is no need for such behaviour, for there is nothing low or despicable about commerce, which is respected in every country. For the wives of the poor, either in town or country, she can only advise hard work and care in the running of their homes.

Apart from advice to different social classes, Christine had some for women in special situations, widows for instance, who find themselves in financial difficulties after the death of their husbands and who in such cases are 'never knowledgeable enough not to be tricked'. This is obviously based on her own hard experience. They must be strong and courageous and not spend their time weeping and moaning. Life had clearly taught her wisdom in this matter. But she had advice too for women in general, obviously gleaned from her own keen observation of her sex, as for instance when she tells older women to be indulgent to young ones, forgiving what their youth makes them say and remembering what they themselves were like when young. They should 'leave young people in peace and not be always criticising them'. Nor should women of different ages be jealous of each other for, she shrewdly says, 'if you no longer have the vices of youth, this is not out of virtue but because your nature no longer inclines you to them; and it is because you can no longer experience them that they seem to you abominable'.

The originality and perception of the advice and observation of which this book is full appear to have made Christine's contemporaries find it a treasure indeed, and ensured for it in one way a greater and more lasting success than the *Cité des Dames* had achieved. For unlike its forerunner it was published no less than three times in the century or so after Christine's death, by different publishers and at such close intervals—in 1497, 1505 and 1536—as to indicate that there was a keen and continuing demand for it.⁴

This popular book was the nineteenth or twentieth complete work, counting the letters on the *Roman de la Rose* as one, that Christine had written between the years 1399 and 1406, in addition to what, in *Lavision*, she had called 'sundry little ditties'—a surprisingly modest way of referring to the many hundreds of *ballades* and other lyrics with which she had begun.⁵ The range of subjects she had treated had been, as we have seen, extraordinarily wide and varied, covering her subtle exploration of the human heart in the grip of love in the lyrics and longer poems, her early moral themes, works like the *Mutacion de Fortune* and the *Chemin de Longue Estude*, where she had ranged over mythology, ancient and contemporary history and geography, and her fascinating study of her own life and gifts in *Lavision*. Her great history of Charles V, by stressing the changes since his days, had obviously increased her patriotic preoccupation with the moral and political state of the country, as she showed in her *Corps de Policie*, making it one of her two main themes. The other was of course her concern with women to which, beginning with her *Epistre au dieu d'Amours* in 1399 and ending with *La Cité* and *Le Trésor*, she had devoted no less than five of her works.

This would have been a considerable output even for a practised writer in the space of some seven or eight years. For Christine who, when she began to write at the age of thirty-five, was quite uneducated and had to devote much time and energy to covering a vast programme of reading, besides learning how to express her ideas, it was little short of astonishing. It is therefore not surprising that for the next two or three years she should have produced nothing, with the possible exception of a few poems. Now forty-four or five, after a period of such intensive work, she had certainly earned a rest. It is possible too that, having already said her say on all the subjects nearest her heart, she deliberately intended to write no more.

There is in fact one very slight piece of evidence that this was so, for it was just at that time that Queen Isabeau, prompted perhaps by those last two books on the subject of women, which had made such a stir, informed Christine that she would like to have copies of all that she had written. As this was virtually a royal command, Christine immediately put the work in hand, and the result was a superb manuscript which subsequently had a fascinating history before coming to rest in the

British Museum where it now is.[6] It consists of 398 leaves, bound in two volumes, its beautiful script (not all in the same hand, for it must have been the work of many scribes) illuminated with quantities of miniatures and vignettes illustrating the texts. It is thought that for these Christine may have employed Anastaise,[7] whose work she had so praised in her *Cité des Dames*; and certainly the ravishing robes, particularly of the women, do suggest that they were the work of a feminine hand. In view of the nature of the queen's command it is not easy to understand why these volumes contain the omissions they do; for although all the love poems, both short and long, are there, the early moral writings too and the *Roman de la Rose* letters, of which we know that Christine had once sent the queen a special copy, she omits *Le Dit de la Rose*, the *Mutacion de Fortune*, the *Fais et bonnes meurs de Charles V*, the *Corps de Policie* and, more surprising still, the work which she had only just completed, the *Trésor*.

On the other hand Christine added in this manuscript not only a few extra lyrics, of which no other copies exist, but a complete series of *ballades* entitled *Cent balades d'amant et de dame*,[8] which is otherwise unknown. Nor is it known when Christine composed these poems, whose subject-matter in some ways resembles that of *Le Duc des Vrais Amants*, relating as it does the lover's long courtship of a lady, the final kindling of her answering love, their mutual grief when he is forced to go abroad, her jealousy when on his return he seems to have changed and fallen in love with another. In the last few of the hundred *ballades*, she is so convinced that he is false that she falls ill and hopes to die, and the series ends with a poem ten pages long called *Lay de Dame*, which is a cry of grief and complaint to the god of love.

It is hardly likely that Christine would have written this series at the same time as that earlier poem whose sentiments it so much resembles. In a preliminary *ballade* of the new series she says that, although at present she has not the heart nor is in the mood to write more 'amorous ditties', she is doing so at the request of one who is so charming that she pleases everyone. Who this 'sweet and debonaire' lady is has of course been a subject of conjecture; the likeliest suggestion is that she was Christine's favourite, Mary of Berry, whose young husband, then Count of Clermont, after the first, passionate years of their courtship and marriage, later proved a fickle character where women were concerned, while Mary remained unswervingly loyal. Knowing how devoted Christine was to her, Mary might have confided her sorrows in her and asked her to enshrine them in verse, of course not for publication, thus making a sort of companion piece to that earlier poem in which the young Count of Clermont had asked her to describe his courtship in its early days. Then, as no names were mentioned in it, Mary might have agreed that Christine should include it in the queen's manuscript.

The only other new work which Christine included in this special manuscript was the dedicatory poem addressed to the queen.[9] It is in this poem that she says 'there is no such lovely occupation' as writing* although she admits that it is an effort, for she speaks also of '*mon labour et lonc travail*'. The whole tone of this poem seems to imply that it was intended not only as a dedication but as a preface to a collected edition of her works. This is our one slender piece of evidence that she intended to write no more, although it only makes it more puzzling that she should have omitted some of her most important compositions from these magnificent volumes.

We do not know when they were completed and presented to the queen, but they must have taken a year or two to prepare, during which Christine would have had to oversee the work. At the same time she was having another beautifully illumined manuscript, this time only of her poems, prepared for the Duke of Berry,[10] who already had copies of her prose works, which she had presented to him over the years as New Year's gifts. Berry's volume included another new poem, this time in the form of a valedictory poem at the end of it, again addressed to the queen and dated 'two days before Candlemas 1407' (1408, new dating). Berry had always rewarded Christine handsomely for these offerings, and for this latest and most beautiful of them he gave her the magnificent sum of two hundred *écus*. Since such was the custom, no doubt the queen was equally if not more generous, especially as it must have cost Christine a great deal to have the manuscript made.

It is probable that she was therefore at last in a better financial position than she had been since the death of her husband, so we may imagine her almost for the first time since her widowhood enjoying life in Paris, where she was now a well-known figure. Even at the time of her letters on the *Roman de la Rose* she had, as we know, a reputation in university and court circles. And the poet Eustache Deschamps had a high regard for her. But there is also some contemporary evidence

* See page 77 above.

that she was gradually becoming even more widely known. A certain Mathieu Tomassin, who later became a councillor to Charles VII, remarked in his *Registre Delphinal* that he often saw her about in the streets of Paris, which gives the impression that she was a familiar sight.[11] Another witness is Guillebert de Metz, whose description of Paris has already been quoted. Speaking of the city as he remembers it in 1407, he says there were sixty thousand scholars and professional men, musicians and writers, among whom he particularly names *'damoiselle Christine de Pisan, qui dictait toutes manières de doctrines et divers traités'*.[12] And as he then goes straight on to talk of the courts of love, at which all manner of love songs were sung, we may assume that these included some by Christine, so that her name would be familiar also to the musicians and gallants who competed there.

Most striking of all is the testimony of Martin Le-Franc, who was at one time secretary to Pope Nicolas V. Himself a great defender of women, many of whom in France, he says 'put men to shame both in the fields and the cities', he writes charmingly of Christine in his *Champion des Dames*, one of the most celebrated poems of the fifteenth century, which he dedicated to Philip the Good of Burgundy in 1440.[13] Her renown, he says 'is very fresh and bright' and her name 'is unceasingly trumpeted everywhere'. He cannot praise her enough, for truly she had 'all the flowers in her lovely garden'. He praises her great contemporaries too, Froissart, Machaut, Alain and others, but Christine was the equal of Cicero and Cato, the latter for wisdom and the former for eloquence, of which she was 'the rose and the bud'. To write thus only a few years after her death he must surely have been well aware of her at this time of her widest renown.

There is even an echo in some of Christine's own words that she had latterly been finding life more agreeable, for at the end of her *Corps de Policie*, written in 1406, she had suddenly and surprisingly said that of all the nations in the world, France was the best country to live in, partly because 'there are no such benign princes nor so human as there are there', but also because of the courtesy and amiability of its people.

But alas, this period when she was at last able to taste the fruits of her labours and to enjoy a little leisure was to be brutally cut short. And if it was happiness that had made it seem a suitable time for silence, it can only have been shock and grief at the terrible event which ended it, followed by desolation and despair, that literally struck her dumb for another two years. On the evening of November 23rd, 1407, Louis of

Orleans went to visit the queen, who was staying, as she often did, at the Hôtel Barbette, a private residence of hers in that part of Paris now called the Marais. While he was there, at about eight o'clock in the evening, a messenger arrived, alleging that he came from the king, who urgently wanted to see his brother at the Hôtel de Saint Pol. Louis, suspecting nothing and always ready to obey the brother who was so good to him, left at once and, with a handful of retainers, rode down the Vieille Rue du Temple, as it was then called, singing to himself and swinging a glove. As he came abreast of a house called the House of the Image, a band of ruffians with their horses burst out of it and attacked him. Startled at the noise they made, the horses of his own retainers bolted and left him with only a page on foot. At a loss to understand this assault Louis called out that he was the Duke of Orleans. They answered that he was the man they wanted, whereupon they hacked off the hand that held the reins, dragged him from his mule, stabbed him with their swords and cleft his head in two with their axes. They then set fire to the house in which they had hidden, mounted their horses and rode off at top speed, leaving Louis lying in the road among his blood and spilt brains, with only one torch to illuminate the grisly sight.

The news of this appalling murder quickly brought the Provost of Paris, Guillaume de Tignonville, to the scene. And when it reached the princes of the blood they ordered him to institute enquiries without delay and to begin a house to house search for the criminals. But the enquiries soon proved unnecessary for only three days later, when the Council was sitting at the Hôtel de Saint Pol, John the Fearless, knowing that the assassins, who were lodged in his Hôtel d'Artois, would soon be found, brazenly confessed that it was he who had plotted and arranged all the details of the crime. Moreover he expressed no shame for his guilt and pretended to no remorse. Having spoken he left the meeting, and left Paris, too, to return to his own lands, knowing himself so powerful that it was unlikely that his old uncles and the other princes, and certainly not the feeble king, would take action against him.

The effect on Christine of hearing all this is not hard to imagine. The shock of hearing that Louis, her paragon of princes, had been so hideously done to death must have been even greater for her to realise than it was for Nicolas de Baye, the clerk of the *Parlement*, who wrote, as though he could hardly believe it, that that night he who, at about eight o'clock, was the Duke of Orleans, the lord of wide lands, 'is now ashes and putrefaction'. Then too there was the horror of learning that it was another of her 'benign princes' who had done this deed. The fact that she never praises him, as she had so often praised his father, nor even mentions him, perhaps indicates that she had no particular liking for John the Fearless. The knowledge, which she must have had, that he was no friend to Louis, would have been enough to account for that. Even so, he had been a benefactor to her, taking an interest in her writings and compensating her generously for the manuscripts of them she gave him.

But the conflict of personal feelings which this horrible murder must have aroused in the heart of Christine, the woman and the writer, was not to be compared with the foreboding it could not but have created in the mind of Christine the patriot and the prophet. For the threat of civil war which she had foreseen in 1405, when she had tried to prevent it and there was still time to do so, was now obviously past averting. And just as she had foreseen then that such a war must inevitably bring in its train the far greater danger of foreign invasion, so now her clear and prophetic mind may well have foreseen that such an invasion had become more likely still, and would lead to the disintegration of the France that all her life she had known and loved, until in the end it was brought to utter ruin.

It was not to be long now before she had far more reason to lament 'all my good days are over' than she had when she first thought so in the early days of her widowhood. For throughout the years to come, heralded by the death of Louis, most of the great ones whom she had admired and who had helped her were to depart from the world, as well as some of the chief officials who had been her friends since her youth, leaving her more and more alone. The doom began to fall swiftly. In December 1408, only a year after the death of Louis, his wife Valentina, heartbroken by the loss of her husband and by her failure to obtain justice against his murderer from his brother the king, died at Blois, leaving her fourteen-year-old son Charles to avenge his father, with the help of all the remaining princes of the *fleur-de-lis*. But Charles, though courageous, was young and inexperienced, and his allies not particularly warlike, while Burgundy was powerful, ruthless and a wily schemer, able to twist the poor mad king round his finger to the point of making him forgive him for his brother's murder.

Armed with the royal favour, Burgundy began to strengthen his influence in Paris by persuading the king to dismiss two of the great officials who had always befriended Christine. The first of these was Guillaume de Tignonville, the Provost of Paris, to whom she had appealed during the debate on the *Roman de la Rose*. He had been a supporter of Louis of Orleans, so Burgundy had him replaced by a creature of his own, Pierre des Essarts. But at least he left him alive. A worse fate awaited another of her friends at court, Jean de Montagu, the Grand Master of the King's Household. Pierre des Essarts arrested him, presumably on Burgundy's orders, on a charge of having abetted Louis of Orleans, and after undergoing terrible tortures he was hanged, his headless body being subsequently left on the gibbet for three years for all to see. The shock caused by this latest appalling exploit of Burgundy's made it clear to the allied princes that they must now fight not merely to avenge Louis but to defend the kingdom against his plots and his overweening ambition.

The menace of conflict that now filled the air made it impossible for so active a spirit as Christine's to keep silent any longer. She must take action whether it could help or not. And since her only weapon was her pen, she now took it up again. But what could she turn it to but the one subject that filled men's minds: war? It was a subject that had produced a good deal of literature from Roman times onwards. Three Latin works were well known in the Middle Ages: the *Stratagemata* of Frontinus, the *Facta Dictaque Memorabilia* by Valerius Maximus, but above all the *De Re Militari*, of Vegetius, which had been translated by Jean de Meun under the title of *L'Art de Chevalerie*. There was also a book called *L'Arbre des Batailles*, by Honoré Bonet, a contemporary of Christine's.

She might have thought that all these books had between them already covered the ground sufficiently. But as each treated different aspects of the subject it seemed to Christine that there was room for another which should combine them all and bring them up to date. She gave this as her aim at the beginning of the book she now began to write and which she called *Le Livre des fais d'armes et de chevalerie*.* She excuses herself for her boldness in treating such an important theme, of which she knew she was not worthy because of 'the lytylhed of my persone'. It was not presumption or arrogance which had

---

* There is no modern critical edition of this book. The quotations from it in this chapter are taken from Caxton's translation of it, on which see the Appendix *Christine and England*, below, page 165.

impelled her to it, she said, but her wish to help those noble men who followed the profession of arms. As such men are not usually clerks versed in subtle language she intended to write as plainly as she could. The success of her past writing encouraged her to feel she had the ability to do so. And finally she begged the 'noble state of Chivalrye' not to take it amiss that a woman should treat of such a subject, but to think of what was said rather than who said it.

Woman though she was, few contemporary writers could have had the patience and the skill to make a better job of what she frankly admitted was largely a compilation of the work of others. But she did not merely repeat what others had written. With her lively mind she mastered her material to the point where she was able to judge it, with the result that she sometimes disagreed with her predecessors and could add a criticism or comment of her own in which we can recognise that shrewd common sense of hers. Nor did she forget the circumstances in which she was writing, for she began by repeating what she had already said in her *Lavision* concerning the causes for which fighting is lawful and those for which it is not. She condemns war to wreak vengeance but approves of it to uphold justice, thus obliquely supporting the recently enlarged aims of the allied princes.

As she had to make use of so much material she divided her book this time into four parts instead of her customary three, and for the first two she relied largely on her Roman authors. But there is a certain amount, too, of more immediate interest, describing conditions in her own times. She says, for instance, that when the king himself does not go to war (as Charles V did not) he must be replaced by the constable with two marshals under him. Her account of the qualities a good constable should have describes a paragon of knightly virtues and one wonders whether the Lord of Albret, who then held that office and whom she had always admired, was the model for her picture. He must be neither hasty nor hot-tempered, 'rightful in justice, benygne in conversation . . . of lytyl words . . . hardy, sure and diligent, not covetous, fyers to his enemyes, pyetous to them that he vanquissed and to them that be under hym . . . not lightly angry'. She describes the qualities that make good soldiers too and how they should be treated in all circumstances. She goes into the business of choosing camp sites and the drawing up of troops in preparation for battle. This leads to the question of stores that will be needed in a campaign—bedding, victuals, wine and, rather surprisingly, vinegar to drink in summer—and to the weapons both for defence and assault: powder, stones, guns, timber and cords—for which latter, again rather surprisingly, if in short supply, women's hair is useful! When the practical problems of assaulting castles and towns is raised, Christine, seeming to foresee the coming English invasion, says that she has consulted certain 'wyse knyghtes' who are expert. She hopes that those who read what they have told her will not, because of 'the feebleness of a lytyl paper', despise 'thys fayre ordinaunce' that might be 'socourable namely in thyse royalme yf the case in tyme to come befel'. She ends her second section with a fascinating account of how those extraordinary assault machines, in use from Roman times until the Middle Ages, were constructed, manned and operated.

The subjects of the last two parts of her book were the laws that govern both the military and civilians in time of war. Her source for this was the book called *L'Arbre des Batailles*, which Honoré Bonet had written in 1387 or 1388 and dedicated to Charles VI. Bonet had only died in 1400, and as he was a fervent admirer of Louis and Valentina of Orleans, this had obviously endeared him to Christine, who knew him well. She was thus able to hit upon a lively framework which enabled her to use a combination of his views and her own, for she pretends, as was her wont, that he appeared before her in a dream. Addressing her as 'dere love crystine', he said he had come to help her in her work by suggesting that she should cut some of the branches of his tree, taking the best and using the timber as a foundation for an edifice of her own. When Christine feared that she might be rebuked for this, he told her it was a common usage among his disciples, for by thus making a work more widely known, the more authentic it becomes. The skill lies in using the borrowings rightly. He was sure Christine would do this, and he could certify that many a wise man would commend her work.

This important justification of the medieval habit of plagiarism encouraged Christine to set to work and ask him no fewer than seventy-three questions, sometimes agreeing with his answers, but sometimes convincing him with her contrary views. A great many of the laws concern the treatment of ordinary soldiers, their pay and conditions, and contain such remarks as that prisoners should never be killed or made to labour. As for ordinary civilians in time of war, labourers or shepherds for example, they should never be taken prisoner; they did not want the war and so should not suffer for it. Women and children should never be held to ransom, a rule that made Christine burst out 'thenne is not this daye this law wel kept'.

More interesting are questions concerning travellers and foreign civilians in time of war. For instance, if an Englishman comes to Paris to get a degree when England and France are at war, and a Frenchman takes him prisoner and brings him before a judge, can the Englishman plead a privilege granted to scholars in the time of Charlemagne, or is the Frenchman justified in thinking that, as he had no safe-conduct, he might be a spy? Christine thinks a true scholar ought never to be taken prisoner, and this privilege should extend to his servants also, if he has any with him. What is more, if he falls sick in Paris, his kinsmen have the right to visit him, for 'more grete is the ryght of nature than is the ryght of werre'. The reference to safe-conducts causes Christine to wonder how anybody can trust them 'seeyng the lytel trouthe and fydelyte that this day renneth thrughe al the worlde'. Moreover they are often traps for the unwary, unless they state clearly that they cover not only 'sauff gooying but sauff comyng ayen and also sauf abydyng'.

The last few pages of her book are devoted to the subject of heraldry, on which Christine questions Bonet and reports the answers he gives her. This is a most interesting section and covers not only the wearing of coats of arms in battle but the painting of such blazons on banners and pennants. We are told how these customs first started, which persons have the legal right to use arms—all in the greatest detail—and there is a final fascinating paragraph on the colours of heraldry. Gold is the most noble, red or purple, representing fire, which only princes may use, is the second, azure, for air, is the third, and the fourth is white, after which come black, and last green. A passing remark of interest is that gold, the metal presumably, is given by 'masters of physic' as 'a sovereign comfort to a man debilitated and near death'. Although Christine was quoting Bonet for much of all this, it was she who, as he had prophesied, subsequently came to be regarded as a considerable authority on this whole question, especially in England.

Bonet had, as we know, told Christine that he was sure her book would be commended by many wise men; but there is no evidence that it caused much of a stir among her immediate contemporaries. Of the twenty manuscripts which exist, most are later than her own lifetime and only nine of them mention her name as author.[14] One printed version appeared fifty years after her death, again not mentioning her name, which was similarly omitted from another, a poor reprint of the first, which came out early in the sixteenth century.[15] Yet Bonet's prophecy was in the end fulfilled, for the time was to come when her book received greater praise, and from a more illustrious personage, in another country than her own, than any of her other works had done; and because of him it was publicised in a way that would surely have been beyond the imagining either of Bonet or of Christine herself.*

* See Appendix *Christine and England*, below, page 165.

CHAPTER FOURTEEN

Fulfilment

ALTHOUGH Christine probably began her *Fais d'Armes* in the winter of 1409 when civil war first seemed imminent, except for that one sentence when she remarked that what she said about assaulting towns might be useful if such a situation ever came to pass in France, she seems to have regarded the book more as a background work in the spirit of the times than as one for which there was an immediate need. And as such a compilation obviously demanded a great deal of preliminary reading and much labour in its composition, it is not surprising that it apparently took her two or three years to complete. This we gather from the fact that it was not until January 1st, 1413, that it formed her customary new year's gift of a manuscript of her latest work to the Duke of Berry.[1]

But now that she had begun to write again, she soon thought of other subjects. First she wrote a curious little work at the request of Charles the Noble, King of Navarre, a prince she never otherwise mentions. We know of no reason why he asked her to do it, but that he did so is another proof of how well-known as a writer she had become. She called it *Sept Psaumes allegorisés* and it consists of extracts from what are known as the seven penitential psalms, to which she appended meditations and prayers. The meditations are in a more or less conventionally pious style, but the prayers are of interest because in them she names many of the familiar figures of her history. She begins with the dead Charles V and Philip of Burgundy, but rather strangely makes no mention of Louis of Orleans; with them she mentions her own parents and other benefactors, and prays too that God will give her 'the gift of counsel' so that she can helpfully use it—a prayer obviously already granted. Next she prays for the queen, that she may live 'as a good example', a necessary prayer indeed, and then for the descendants of Charles V, including of course Berry and John the Fearless and also Charles of Navarre 'by whose command and wish this present work is made'. She then

147

goes on to pray for all the inhabitants of the kingdom, clerks and students of the University of Paris, justices, burgesses and merchants, including rather unexpectedly 'all those sent on embassies from France to make peace anywhere'.[2]

There is no particular feeling in these pious prayers, which were written during the last six months of 1409, that they were called forth by any immediate danger. The same is not true of an impassioned cry she wrote a year later, in August 1410, which she called *Lamentation sur les maux de la guerre civile*.[3] This recalls that letter which she had written to the queen five years earlier, when civil war first threatened. But now that that threat was so much greater, Christine's appeal to those who might avert it is infinitely more eloquent and anguished, as one feels from her opening words when she describes how, sitting alone as she started to write, the tears so clouded her eyes and ran down her face on to the paper that she could hardly find a dry space on which to write, so much the bitter drops smudged her words. That this was no mere figure of speech seems to be proved when, half-way through, carried away by her own heart-rending words, she says again that she has to keep laying down her pen in order to wipe the unceasing tears from her eyes.

Her appeal this time was addressed to all those with any power to avert the war, beginning with the princes who, as she must have heard, were at that moment planning to write to the king to tell him that they intended to take up arms in order to help him to restore good government and put down violence. She begs them to see the evils that must come of civil war: the ruined cities and castles, the slain bodies of divided families lying in the uncultivated fields, the ensuing famine followed by the rebellion of the hungry people. And what good ever came of a victory in such a cause, she sensibly asks. When she turns to the queen, whose uselessness she now clearly realises, a contemptuous note rings in her voice as she calls to her 'Crowned queen of France, are you asleep? What is preventing you from stopping this mortal enterprise?' And she goes on to ask what the king's council are doing, and what the clergy, who should be marching in processions with devout prayers. 'Ah, France, France, once so glorious a kingdom', she cries. Her final appeal is to the Duke of Berry, asking him how he, 'the most noble uncle now living', can bear to see his nephews assembled for mortal battle against their own flesh, remembering as he must the great natural love between their parents, his dead brothers and sisters.

Paris, the city of his father, where he himself was born, cries to him with tears and sighs, begging him to make peace.

She ends by calling herself 'a poor voice crying in this kingdom, desirous of peace and the good of all of you, your servant Christine, who prays that she may see the day when peace comes'. And she dates her letter August 23rd, 1410. Whether that day had any particular significance in history we do not know. But it is more than likely that what induced Christine to write her appeal then was that she had just heard of the death, a few days earlier, of the old Duke of Bourbon. This tender-hearted old man had virtually retired from public life in the previous October, when he had left Paris at the time of the arrest of Jean de Montagu, too sickened with horror to remain there while he was being tortured and executed. A few months later he had decided to go and end his days in a monastery he had founded at Vichy, and there on August 17th he died. What is almost conclusive proof that it was the news of this that had impelled Christine to write her appeal then was her reference in it to the Duke of Berry as 'the most noble uncle now living'—an unemotional enough statement but one behind which one can sense not only her personal sorrow at the loss of this great noble, but her poignant realisation that now there was only one left of that older generation whose fatherly help and kindness had surrounded her from her earliest youth.

Unfortunately her appeal was written too late to achieve its purpose, for in September the allied princes sent the king the manifesto they had been working on since April. But the only effect it had was that the king gave them no credit for their intentions and ordered them to disperse their troops. They refused to do so until he had heard their case, and as he would not they marched on Paris. Hearing of this, Burgundy collected his troops too and marched to meet them. But as he was apparently not yet ready for battle, probably not having believed in the genuineness of their intentions, he offered terms instead. These only went part way to reform some of the abuses in the state which they desired to correct. But as winter was coming on, when it was customary for fighting to cease, a temporary truce was patched up and both sides returned home.

But the allies were still determined to check Burgundy's manifest intention to rule the kingdom—the king had agreed that the dauphin should be under his care and control, and the people of Paris, we know, were his fervent supporters. So the Orleanists marched again on Paris in September 1411. This time Burgundy was ready and waiting for them, and the fighting that then ensued was as fierce and bloody as Christine had feared it would be. As it took place near Paris, at Saint Cloud and Saint Ouen, the Parisians lived in a constant state of terror, as well as in great economic difficulties. Some of them indeed added to the prevailing tension, for the butchers of Paris, incited it is thought by Burgundy, rose in support of him against the Orleanists, making the city a still more alarming place to live in. At first the allies achieved some success, but in the end Burgundy was victorious and when winter came on again the Orleanists, a large part of whose army had been killed, were forced once again to retire and try to repair their losses.

Undaunted, the allied princes made yet another attempt in the summer of 1412. This time the civil strife threatened to be on a fuller scale than during the previous encounters, for the king and the dauphin joined their forces with those of Burgundy and marched to Bourges, where the Duke of Berry and the warlike Count of Armagnac, who had joined the Orleanist faction in 1409, awaited them. The other allied princes were on their way to join them there, hoping to bring with them some English forces whose help Charles of Orleans had requested. But the battle had hardly been joined before it came to an unexpected end. For the dauphin, now a boy of fifteen, suddenly declared that the war had gone on long enough and it would be better if his uncles and cousins united to help him govern the kingdom, as he would increasingly have to do because of his father's illness, rather than fight each other. He therefore proposed that they should all meet at Auxerre in the following August and there make a final peace. Although neither side was pleased at being thus cheated of a possible victory, the royal command had to be obeyed and the meeting therefore took place and peace was signed on August 22nd.

One would have imagined that someone with as much knowledge of the issues at stake and political sense as Christine would have foreseen that it was a peace unlikely to endure; for the sincerity and justice of the allied cause had not been recognised and nothing had been done to check Burgundy's ambition. But for her, peace instead of civil war was so much the overriding consideration that she whole-heartedly rejoiced at it. And what delighted her more than the actual peace was that it was the dauphin, the Duke of Guienne as she generally called him, who had decreed it and carried it through. She had, as we know,

latterly been hoping that perhaps he would in time emulate his grandfather, and now he seemed to be showing the first signs of this.

So full of all this was she that one almost suspects that she was
present at Auxerre and saw him presiding over the proceedings. For on
September 1st, only a week after the treaty was signed, she began to
write her *Livre de la Paix*, addressed to him. She obviously wrote her
opening pages under the stress of great emotion, for she begins in an
excitable way, calling the dauphin at one and the same time a high and
noble prince, already acting like a mature man at the age of fifteen, and
an 'inspired child'. He deserves to be called Louis the God-given,
through whom God has shown his mercy to France. She begs him not
to despise her. She has woven for him a crown of beautiful wild flowers
'to adorn the head of your pleasant youth', while he is waiting for 'the
crown of royal dignity'.

With this rather fulsome beginning Christine introduces the serious
purpose of her book, for the flowers with which she planned to crown
the dauphin were the seven kingly virtues that had adorned his grandfather, Charles V. She knew that, brought up as the young man had
been, a prey to conflicting influences and left much to his own devices,
he had had little or none of that moral training that in the *Corps de
Policie* she had said was essential for a future ruler. So although she had
already written of the virtues of Charles V, she proposed repeating
much of what she had then said for the benefit of the dauphin; and by
describing the conduct to which the proper use of those virtues should
lead, she managed to slip in instances of the dauphin's misuse of them
and thus painted a lively portrait of the rather spoilt young man he
was, and the people who surrounded him. Thus in talking of the first
virtue of prudence, she stresses that it should lead its possessor, as it had
led Charles V, to surround himself with wise and good councillors
whose qualities she describes. They need not necessarily be old—some
old men are silly, she says—but they should never indulge their lord by,
for instance, mocking others at a banquet just to make him laugh.
They should rather gently restrain any such tendency on his part.

So intent was Christine on instilling prudence into the dauphin that
she devoted the whole of the first part of her book to this one virtue
alone. She had written it at top-speed and finished it in November. But
within that short space of two months the state of the country so
worsened, and as a result the seething discontent of the people so
increased, that she felt it impossible to go on with her work for the

time being 'because of the broken peace', she says. The actual fighting between the princes had, it is true, stopped for the time being. But those butchers of Paris, whom Burgundy had encouraged to rise in support of him, having tasted blood, as it were, now took matters into their own hands and formed themselves into a citizen army under their own leader, a skinner of beasts called Caboche. Their aim was no less than the reform of all the abuses from which they suffered. It will be remembered that it was these abuses that the Orleanists, in their manifesto of 1410, had begged the king in vain to let them reform. Now, ironically enough, Burgundy, always quick to seize any advantage, persuaded the Cabochiens that it was the Orleanists who were responsible for them, and urged them to attack them and their supporters, even at times himself joining them in the veritable reign of terror that then began, when they burst into the houses of many nobles, even of the dauphin, taking some prisoners and killing others. Soon they were in complete control of the city, whose gates they guarded.

But by the summer of 1413 this violence started to recoil on itself. The burgesses and merchants began to see that Burgundy was largely responsible for what had happened and to turn against him. At a wedding at the end of July, which was attended not only by the king and the dauphin but by the young Charles of Orleans, he seized the opportunity once again to offer the services of himself and his allies to quell the terror. This offer was at last accepted; another peace, the Peace of Pontoise, was signed, and on September 1st the dauphin, accompanied by the Orleanists and their army, entered Paris in a splendid state procession, to be welcomed by the citizens with great rejoicing. The Cabochiens were forced to surrender their prisoners and were themselves either imprisoned or banished. Burgundy prudently absented himself from Paris.

No one could have welcomed the return of the dauphin with his new allies to Paris with more relief than did Christine. The proof is that on September 3rd, only two days later, she began work on her *Livre de la Paix* again. She opens the second part by praising the princes, and especially the dauphin, for putting an end to the reign of terror, and then takes up again the theme of the princely virtues he will need to restore the social order. Having spent so long on the first of those virtues, prudence, she treats more briefly the remaining six: justice, magnanimity, force (by which she means strength of character), clemency or benignity, liberality and truth. Once again she reveals how far the dauphin still was from a true understanding of these virtues, when she tells him that liberality must not be confused with extravagance and prodigality (to which he was prone); it meant being quick to notice and help those in need, as his grandfather did. Then again, to be clement or benign one must know how to listen patiently and indulgently to humble people, not answering hastily or giving vent to anger. Sometimes she was bold enough to give the young prince good advice which she must have known he needed, unconnected with the virtues under discussion. He must not be 'solitary', she says, by which she means that he must not prefer his private pleasure to his public duties, and above all must not indulge in foolish pursuits or in voluptuous pleasure.

One cannot help wondering how the dauphin who, we know, did not brook criticism easily, liked this admonishing tone. Perhaps it did not come as a surprise to him, for she refers in one curious passage to a little treatise called the *Advision du Coq*,[4] apparently on the subject of the danger of envy in a prince, which she says she had presented 'to you yourself, Louis of France, sitting in your room at Saint Pol in Lent of this year'. This seems to indicate that Christine, now a woman of fifty, had gained such a privileged position that she was allowed to speak her mind even to the dauphin. Perhaps too he did not take her too seriously, for it cannot be denied that towards the end of this book she shows a certain prosiness, repeating at too great length her old stories of Charles V, saying from time to time 'as I have already said' and asking the dauphin's pardon if she is rather prolix.

Of greater interest than this lesson in virtues is what Christine says in the last two parts of her book about what she calls 'the mad government of the small and bestial people'. She had, as we know from her *Corps de Policie* and scattered remarks in other works, always felt strongly that, although the common people were a valuable part of the state, they should always be kept in their place. Her recent experience of the terrors of mob rule had turned this firm though comparatively mild opinion into violently anti-democratic views, to which she here gives voice again and again. Men may be born equal, she says, but it always immediately becomes apparent that the upper classes have better manners and more courage than the lower. The poor must remain in the state to which God has called them, humble before their betters and doing their work loyally. If they absent themselves or refuse to work they must be thrown into prison. The people may have a natural tendency to think they are badly governed and ought to rebel, but it is folly for them to do so for they can never succeed for long. How can labourers who know nothing and can barely say their prayers govern others? To see such people's behaviour in positions of power, based on what they have seen in comedies, is laughable.

Besides the folly of it there is the danger that such people, if they gain power, finding that they outnumber the other classes may start a civil war between them. It was clearly her dread of this, during the recent terror, that inspired her present diatribe. 'O God,' she says, 'where is the heart that does not tremble thinking of that perilous adventure when this kingdom was nearly lost' because of what she calls 'the diabolic common people'. She admits she was terrified and she calls on the princes never to forget the horror of it. Returning to the main purpose of her book she tells the dauphin she has not brought all this up to set him at odds with the people, of whom she knows there are many that such exploits grieve, but to make him see how necessary it is to govern well and not give the people cause for discontent.

Christine wrote Le Livre de la Paix, which was to be her last major work, even more quickly than was her wont, for according to her custom she presented a manuscript of it to the Duke of Berry as a new year's gift on January 1st, 1414. During the following year, the book did not justify its title or her hopes, except in so far as the behaviour of the dauphin was concerned. For Burgundy made two more attempts to renew the civil war, first in March, when he marched on Paris with his forces hoping the butchers would again rise and join him, but was repulsed by the dauphin and his allies, and again later in the summer when he mounted a campaign near Arras. The royalist and allied troops were on the point of winning this when Burgundy suddenly surrendered. Another peace was signed and the Orleanists returned to Paris to enjoy a pleasant and peaceful winter there.

One of the greatest events of that winter must have given peculiar satisfaction to Christine, for in January 1415 the king had his murdered brother Louis' obsequies solemnly celebrated in Notre Dame, at a service attended not only by most of the allied princes but by a great throng of the citizens of Paris, who had been his enemies when he lived. Christine's old friend Jean Gerson, Chancellor of the University of Paris, preached the sermon, praising Louis unreservedly for his gifts and qualities and publicly stating that John of Burgundy, the written defence of whose crime had already been burnt the year before, ought to be humiliated by being made to recognise his crime in public.

Burgundy was of course far too powerful for this ever to be enforced, and so far from repenting of his past conduct he was meanwhile continuing his disloyal and ambitious career by negotiating with Henry V of England, who that winter was preparing to renew the Hundred Years War. After a long-drawn-out exchange of letters and embassies, in an attempt to put the blame for this on the French king, Henry invaded France in August 1415 and besieged Harfleur. The French were ill-prepared for this attack, not having believed that Henry really intended a serious invasion. So the siege only lasted three weeks, and although the small English army suffered many losses, they were victorious and Harfleur fell. As all this happened so quickly it is quite possible that the ordinary citizens of Paris, Christine among them, were unaware of what had occurred, and felt no cause for alarm if they heard thereafter that Henry and his greatly reduced army, whose soldiers were much weakened by dysentery through fighting in the August heat, were marching across the north of France on their way to Calais and home. The news that the king and the dauphin were at last assembling an army to try and defeat them before they got there, and that nearly all the great feudatories and their military vassals had responded to their call, so that an immense army had been gathered, was enough to breed a feeling of confidence in the country at large, and in the wives of these great princes. So they must have been quite unprepared for the terrible news that they were soon to hear.

Unfortunately a still greater sense of confidence filled that huge French army, finally numbering some fifty or sixty thousand, when, after marching for some weeks along parallel routes to the English, they at last came up with them near Maisoncelle and saw what a puny force, of a few hundreds only, they were. They camped within ear-shot of each other on October 24th, the night before the battle, when the silence of the English camp, where the sick, hungry and weary English soldiers spent the night praying or trying to sleep, contrasted with the noise and bustle of the French one, where the nobles in particular, in the highest spirits, and certain of victory, passed the time in jesting and boasting of the valiant deeds they meant to do the next day. So sure of themselves were they that, when it dawned, although the choice of the field was theirs, as the aggressors, they selected a narrow space, hemmed in by woods near the castle of Agincourt, where there was no room to deploy their vast army. But they felt no need to do so, for their plan was to attack in a solid mass of serried ranks of mounted knights, jostling each other in their characteristic eagerness to be first to come to grips with the enemy. But they reckoned without the brilliant skill of the English archers, and the guile of Henry V who had ordered his soldiers to protect them with a close-set hedge of sharpened wooden stakes, driven deep into the ground at an angle slanting towards the oncoming French. So when the mounted knights charged they were first met by a continuous hail of arrows which pierced their armour so that they fell dead or wounded to the ground. Many of their horses were pierced too, while those who survived, charging on, were wounded or gored to death on those terrible sharp spikes, throwing such of their riders as were still mounted. So by the end of the day the field was one mass of dead or wounded, screaming and trampling horses, amid which ten thousand of the flower of the French chivalry lay in their blood, either dead or wounded too, or if still alive unable to rise because of their cumbersome armour, so that they were easily taken captive.

It was now just ten years since Christine, in October 1405, had warned Queen Isabeau that if civil strife broke out between the princes, the time might come when the kingdom would be so weakened that it would be an easy prey to a foreign invader. And now that warning had been fulfilled. But even the prophetic mind of Christine, with its vivid sense of the horrors of war, could hardly have foreseen the terrible holocaust of the battle of Agincourt. So great was the disaster that it heralded a period, lasting over fifty years, when France was reduced almost to the lowest depths in her history.

Some of her favourites vanished from the scene then. The Constable, Charles of Albret, to whom she had written admiring *ballades* when he was a young defender of the cause of women, was among the killed, while Marshal Boucicaut, who had founded the Order of the *Ecu Vert à la Dame Blanche* for the same purpose, was taken prisoner, as was Mary of Berry's husband, the Duke of Bourbon. Captive with them went the young Charles of Orleans, whom Christine must have known, at least slightly, although she never mentions him. Only two months after the battle, at which the dauphin Louis had been present, he died in Paris, of what illness is not known, and with him died all those enthusiastic hopes for the future that Christine had so enthusiastically pinned on him. Of all her old supporters only the Duke of

VII Christine presents her writings to Queen Isabeau. The volume is now Harleian MS 4431. *Photo British Library.*

VIII The three goddesses appear to Christine. Rectitude helps Christine to build the City of Ladies. Harleian MS 4431.

Photo British Library.

Berry remained, but he was now seventy-three, so it was not surprising
that in the following year he too died, the last survivor of the great days
of Charles V.

There could hardly have been any noblewoman in France who did
not suffer losses at Agincourt, but it is unlikely that any had been more
cruelly stricken than Mary of Berry. Although John of Burgundy had
disloyally stayed away from the battle, his two brothers, Anthony,
Duke of Brabant and Philip, Count of Nevers, who were killed there,
were both cousins of hers, while Philip was her son-in-law too.
Among the prisoners Charles of Orleans was a cousin of hers and
Charles, Count of Eu, was her son by an early marriage. But the
cruellest separation of all for her was that from her imprisoned husband
John, Duke of Bourbon; for not only did she deeply love him but she
had to bear the knowledge that, although he had been a brave soldier,
he proved himself too weak a character to endure the slow misery of
captivity and strove by every possible means to obtain his freedom,
treasonably offering to transfer his allegiance to Henry V, to hand over
two of his young sons as hostages, and also paying an enormous sum to
buy his release. Although Mary may not have heard the full details of
all these offers, she was inevitably involved in the struggle to find the
money John was offering, since it was she who now had to administer
their great estates (thus proving how right Christine had been in her
Trésor de la Cité des Dames when she had warned great ladies to prepare
themselves for just such work in the absence of their husbands in the
wars). For such business the experience of the duke, her father, would
have been invaluable, so that his death six months after Agincourt was
the more cruel.

Mary had always been so good to Christine ever since the days of her
early struggles, and the duke, her father, had so helped her with
generous payments in return for her manuscripts (forty-one of which
he left to his daughter by his will) that after his death Christine added
one more to these by sending Mary a letter, to thank her for what she
called her 'large charity' and to try and console her for the losses she had
suffered. As these were so great as to be virtually past consolation, there
was little comfort she could offer beyond the sort of arguments and
beliefs that the normally pious person of the time would hold; and so it
was on these that Christine first dwelt in her letter, which she called
L'Epistre de la prison de vie humaine,[5] striving to show Mary that
those who had died were blessed in that they had escaped from the

prison of earthly life and so were spared the physical and mental degradation of old age. And because they had died fighting for their country they were sure of going to Paradise where they would enjoy peace for all eternity, waiting for their families to join them. So, thinking on these things, Mary must restrain those tears she so often saw on her face now.

It was less easy to console her for the loss of her imprisoned husband and son. Christine may have heard something of Bourbon's behaviour, to judge by her remark that she knows that there have been difficult things for Mary's 'loyal and loving heart' to bear. She can only assure her that if she prays and is patient, God will let her see both of them again—an assurance that was to prove vain for, alas, He never did.

More likely to fortify the strong and fine character that Mary undoubtedly possessed was Christine's reminder of the exceptional advantages she had always enjoyed: a grand-daughter of a king of France, endowed from birth with beauty, health and strength, gifted by nature with a good understanding, reason and wisdom, blessed by fortune with position, power and wealth and married to the 'good and beautiful' Duke of Bourbon. Although she had lost a son by her second marriage, she still had her daughters by that marriage, beside the three young sons that John of Bourbon had given her. Remembering these things and thinking of the countless creatures whom God had also made in His own image, but to whom He had given nothing, what could she be but humble and grateful, ready to bear the sorrows that now had come?

Whether or not this epistle comforted Mary when she finally got it, she had to wait a long time for it, for Christine, who mentions that she began it after the death of Berry in June 1416, ends it by begging Mary not to blame her for not finishing it until January 20th, 1418. This, she says, was because of 'many great anxieties and troubles' that had so upset her mind since she began it that they prevented her from finishing it sooner. Her expression 'anxieties and troubles' sounds as if they were personal matters, though what they were we do not know. Perhaps her mother died at that time, for we hear nothing of her since Christine told us she was still alive in 1405. There is also a faint possibility that her son Jean, although she never mentions him, had become a secretary to the king and was therefore, like everyone connected with the court, in a dangerous position as a result of the ever-worsening situation.

For the dauphin Louis had been succeeded by his brother John of

Touraine, who also soon died and was followed by the youngest son, Charles. As he was only fourteen and the king was in one of his bad phases, Queen Isabeau had herself proclaimed regent. This created a dangerous situation, as she had become an adherent of Burgundy's, whose main opponent now was Count Bernard of Armagnac, the last remaining member of the Orleanist faction. He had had himself made Constable and was governing and defending Paris in case Henry V, who had now conquered Normandy, attempted to take the capital. But Bernard was a very stern governor and some of the more fickle citizens began to think they would prefer their old favourite Burgundy. He was of course aware of this and massed his troops outside the city. On the night of May 18th, 1418, the gates were opened to them and they poured into the city, massacring great numbers of people whom they suspected of being Orleanists, Bernard among them. Fortunately the dauphin escaped.

As Christine was well-known as a sympathiser of the Orleanists, she might easily have shared their fate if she had been in Paris during those dreadful days. But having now nothing there left to live for, it is probable that she had left the capital earlier that year, for we have her word for it that in 1418 she went to live in an abbey. She does not say that this was the royal priory of Poissy though there is one slender piece of evidence that it was.[6] But what more likely than that she should choose the place where her daughter had become a nun, so many years before, and where one hopes she still was, the priory that she knew from that joyous visit seventeen years ago. But this time the doors between those two great towers closed on her for good. There is no reason to suppose that she took any kind of vows for, as she told us in *Le Dit de Poissy*, there were comfortable rooms there where secular women dwelt, not subject to the strict conventual rules.

For all that, the place must have inclined its inhabitants to religious thoughts, so it is not surprising that, not long after she settled there, Christine should have written another short work which she called *Heures de contemplation sur la passion de Nostre Seigneur*.[7] This was on the same lines as the *Epistre de la prison de vie humaine* but of wider implication, for she wrote it not for one woman only but, as she said at the outset, 'feeling pity and compassion for all women and maidens ... stricken by tribulations past and present'; and indeed in general, she went on, 'for all those of the feminine sex who might in any way be concerned'. She had, she told them, been moved by 'natural inclination and pure love' to try and comfort those who had lost friends through death or other causes; and to that end she had searched the Holy Scriptures for 'some good thing' that would help them to have patience.

After she had thus done all she now could for her sex she fell silent, a silence that might have lasted for the rest of her life but for the extraordinary happenings that occurred in 1429, when Joan of Arc first raised the seige of Orleans and then took the dauphin Charles to Rheims to be crowned. It was no wonder that when she heard of these triumphant events, justifying her life-long belief in women, Christine laughed, as she vividly says she did in the poem that she then wrote, after she had spent eleven years weeping enclosed in her abbey. In this poem of sixteen verses,[8] although it is quite unlike anything she had written before, we find the old Christine again, full of life and hope now that, as she says, 'the sun has begun to shine again, bringing again the good time that once we knew . . . through a tender virgin'. She cannot conceal her joy that it was to this 'young girl of sixteen' that 'God gave the strength and power to undo the cords that held France in bondage'. 'What an honour for the feminine sex, which it seems that God loves!' She hopes that Charles, now 'King of the French, the seventh of his name' whom she seems to have seen clearly, will be a good sovereign to his people, worthy of her who has led him by the hand to his coronation. So exalted is she by all this that she hopes Joan will one day lead him on a crusade to the Holy Land, even if she should there end her life in glory.

She ended her poem, as she says in the last stanza, on July 31st, 1429*, a fortnight after the coronation, and after that she wrote no more. The year of her death is not known, but one cannot help hoping that she died soon after that swansong, and did not live long enough to hear of the terrible end, so different from her hopes of it, of the maid who had crowned her long belief in women and defeated the enemies of the country she had loved so well. It can be given to few to see in their last years the two causes for which they have striven all their life thus triumphant at the end of it.

One hopes too that Christine, who was so well informed on all those

---

* This exactly contemporary tribute to Joan of Arc, which is I believe the only such mention of her, is surely enough to refute any subsequent doubts concerning the Maid of Orleans and her deeds. It is one of the results of the long neglect of Christine and her works that this poem should still appear to be unknown to the numerous writers on Joan.

events, living as she was in a priory in such close touch with the Court, heard that the nobleman who was one of the first to believe in Joan and her chief helper at Orleans was the brave and gallant Dunois, the bastard son of her much-admired Louis who had helped her to found, so many years before, the fanciful Order for those who believe in women and swear to help them. Dunois could never have been a member of it, even if it had in truth existed, for he was not yet born when it was founded. But in spirit neither his father nor any of his contemporaries could have been a worthier member of the Order of the Rose.

Christine and England

I T will be remembered that early in her widowhood Christine was befriended by the Earl of Salisbury who, in the course of a stay in Paris in 1397, became such a great admirer of her poems that he took her son Jean to England to be brought up in his household. It was thus through Salisbury that Christine's poems came to the knowledge of Henry IV who, as we know, after the execution of Salisbury, offered to take Jean into his own court. So already in the closing years of the fourteenth century the name of Christine as a poetess was familiar at the English court; and throughout the succeeding reigns of four English kings the interest thus created was so intensified as to make it one of the most striking examples we have of French literary influences on England.

The next Englishman who took a particular interest in Christine's works was a different type of man: Sir John Fastolf, who is thought to have been in some ways the original of Shakespeare's Falstaff. A tough soldier, he served in France for nearly thirty years during the Hundred Years War, taking part in many battles, including Agincourt and the siege of Orleans. As he was Master of the Household to the Governor of Normandy, the Duke of Bedford, and one of the executors of his will in 1432, he was in a position to see that famous manuscript of Christine's works which she had had made for Queen Isabeau and which Bedford had bought from the royal library in 1426. Whether or not it was there that he first read Christine's *L'épistre d'Othea la déesse*, he was obviously so impressed by it that when he finally retired to England about the year 1440, at the age of sixty or so, he brought a manuscript of it with him and settled down to enjoy it among other literary studies.

It was presumably to help him do this that his stepson, Stephen Scrope (Fastolf had married the widow of Sir Stephen Scrope) made a translation of the book, for although he does not name his stepfather in his dedication, he calls himself 'your humble son'. But Fastolf's name is not the only omission in this curious manuscript which Scrope called *The Epistle of Othea to Hector, or the Boke of Knyghthode*, for he gives neither Christine's own title of her work, nor does he attribute the work directly to her, stating in a preface that it was compiled by doctors of the University of Paris at the instance and prayer of the 'fulle wyse gentylwoman of Frawnce called Dame Cristine'. Why he should have taken it upon himself to cast doubts on her authorship in this way, when it is almost certain that any manuscript he used would have contained one of Christine's dedicatory poems to one or other of the great nobles to whom she gave copies, can only be due to his involved mind. He had little literary ability and his translation is only of interest as evidence of the interest in Christine's works in England at that time, although it could not have contributed widely to this as it was never printed.[1]

It is unlikely that it played any part in inspiring another English translator of the work, Robert Wyer, who although he said his was a translation of *Lépistre de Othea déesse*, again omitted the name of Christine and gave it the title *The C hystories of Troye*, which he took from the French edition with the same title, *Les cent histoires de troye*, which Philippe Pigouchet had printed in Paris about 1490 (see Chapter IV, note 11 above). Wyer not only translated this book but says that it was printed by himself 'Robert Wyer, dwelling in S. Martynes parysche, at Charyng Crosse. At the sygne of S. John Evangelist besyde the Duke of Suffolks place'.[2] It is a little quarto, with coarse copies of Pigouchet's woodcuts, which though not dated is thought to have appeared about 1540, and may have helped to prolong the popularity of the work into the reign of Henry VIII, although it cannot have done much for Christine's reputation in England.

The opposite is true of a much more serious translation of another of Christine's works which appeared in a much more splendid edition in 1478. The translator this time took his text from Queen Isabeau's manuscript at a time when it was in his possession. For he was Anthony Wydeville, the son of the Duke of Bedford's widow, Jacquette de Luxembourg, who after Bedford's death had married Sir Richard Wydeville. He had been created the first Earl Rivers, and was the father of Elizabeth, Queen of Edward IV. Anthony inherited not only the title Earl Rivers, after his father was beheaded in 1469, but the manuscript, on the flyleaf of which his name appears among the list of owners. He was a cultivated man who obviously had a keen interest in French literature, for the first work he translated was Guillaume de Tignonville's French translation from the Latin of that popular book of the Middle Ages, *Dicta Philosophorum* (see page 79 above) (which he made from a copy of it which de Tignonville had given him on a pilgrimage to Compostela). His English version was, incidentally, the first book to be printed by Caxton, in 1477, under the title *Dictes and Sayengis of the Philosophres.*

Earl Rivers followed this up with a translation of Christine's *Enseignements Moraux* and her *Proverbes Moraux* from the text in the late queen's manuscript. It was a curiously dull choice among the many more interesting texts he could have selected from that famous manuscript. Caxton printed it in 1478 under the title *The Morale Proverbes of Cristyne.*[3] At the end of the text there are two stanzas which would appear to be by Caxton himself and which run:

> Of these sayynges Cristyne was aucteuresse
> Whiche in makyng hadde such Intelligence
> That thereof she was mireur and maistresse
> Here werkes testifie the experience
> In frensch language was writen this sentence
> And thus Englisshed dooth hit rehers
> Antoin Widewylle therl Ryvers.
>
> Go thou litil quayer and recomaund me
> Unto the good grace of my special lord
> Therle Ryvers, for I have enprinted the
> At his comandement, folowyng evry worde
> His copye as his secretaire can recorde.
> At westmestre, of feverer the XX day
> And of kyng Edward the XVII yere vraye

> Enprinted by Caxton
> In feverer the colde season

Not very interesting though this work is, it obviously hit the taste of the time, for a second edition appeared in 1480 and a third was printed by Wynkin de Worde in 1528. Fortunately for him, Earl Rivers was still alive to see the reprint in 1480, but three years later he was beheaded, by Richard III.

Of the many existing manuscripts of Christine's *Fais d'armes et de chevalerie*, three of which are now in the British Museum, one (Royal 15 E VI) forms part of a huge folio volume of romances and poems given to Margaret of Anjou, the daughter of King René, by the Earl of Suffolk,[4] when he was sent to France to conduct her to England for her marriage to Henry VI. This book must therefore have been known at the English court from then on. But whether Henry VII when he succeeded read it in this manuscript or in the printed French text, which was published in Paris in 1488 in a beautiful edition by Antoine Vérard, the book impressed him so much that he sent for Caxton and 'willed him to reduce the book to our English and natural tongue and to put it in imprint'. It is Caxton himself who tells us this, adding that the interview took place in the Palace of Westminster on January 23rd in the fourth year of the king's reign (i.e. 1489). The king's desire for this, he told Caxton, was 'to thende that every gentylman born to armes and all manere men of werre captayns souldyours vytallers and all other should have knowledge how they ought to behave them in the fayttes of werre and of batayles'. Caxton did his best to fulfil this command of the king (whom he calls the king of England and of France) because 'in myn oppinyon it is as necessary a boke and as requysite as ony may be for every estate hye and lowe that entende the fayttes of werre'. He obviously worked very hard for he finished the translation just over five months later, on July 8th, and the book was 'enprinted' on July 13th of the following year, 1490—a wonderfully swift achievement (by modern standards) both as translator and printer, for a man of sixty-eight, as Caxton then was, and in the last year of his life. He gave it the English title *The Book of fayttes of armes and of chyvalrye*.[5]

The next book of Christine's to appear in English was her *Cité des Dames*, in a version by a translator with the surprisingly modern name of Bryan Anslay, in 1520. In this once again she was not mentioned on a title-page, but even though she was thus not publicly acknowledged there could have been no attempt to deny that the book was by her since she proclaims as much over and over again throughout the text.

Apart from the skilful and often amusing rendering of the text the chief interest is to be found on the fourth and following pages, where the printer writes:

The kyndly entente of every gentylman
is the furtheraunce of all gentylnesse.
And to procure in all that ever he can
For to renewe all noble worthynesse.
This dayly is sene at our eye expresse
Of noble men that do endyte and rede
In bokes olde thyr worthy myndes to fede.

So now of late came in my custodye
This foresayd boke by Bryan Anslay
Yoman of the cellar with the eyght kynge Henry
Of gentylwomen the excellence to say,
The which I lyked, but yet I made delay
It to impresse for that it is the guyse
Of people lewde theyr prowesse to dyspyse.

But then I shewed the foresayd boke
Unto my lorde the gentyll Erle of Kente
And hym requyred thereon to loke
With his counsayle to put it in to prente
And he forthwith as ever dylygente
Of ladyes (alrode) to sprede their royall fame
Exhorted me to prynte it in his name.

And I obeying gladly his instaunce
have done my devoyre of it to make an ende
Prayenge his lordshyp with others that yt shall chaunce
On it to rede the fautes for to amende
If ony be for I do fayne intende
Gladly to please, and wylfully remytte
This ordre rude to them that have fresshe wyte.

On the last page the printer states that the book was 'Imprinted at London in Poules chyrchyarde at the Sygne of the Trynyte by Henry Pepwell. In the yere of our lorde MCCCCCXXI. The XXVI day of October. And the XII yere of the reygne of our souerayne lorde kinge Henry the VIII.' Christine would surely have been pleased to know that she had thus enrolled among the admirers of her book in defence of women an aristocrat, a cellarer and an enterprising publisher, even though the bulk of the 'lewd', that is to say ignorant, people remained as unconvinced of their worth as they always have been.

In France, during the century after Christine's death, only four of her works were printed: the *Othea*, the *Fais d'Armes*, the *Trésor* and the *Chemin de Longue Estude*, this last very imperfectly. Thereafter her name sank into oblivion for two centuries. There is no doubt therefore that in that same hundred years she was more honoured in England than in her adopted country, both as moralist, story-teller, military historian and advocate of women, so much so indeed that it is surprising that thereafter her works were forgotten in England too for an even longer period, in fact until the nineteenth century.

Notes

For full titles of the editions of Christine's works, and of other books whose titles are sometimes given only briefly in the following notes, see bibliography.

CHAPTER ONE

1. Fantuzzi, *Notizie degli scrittori bolognesi*, Vol. VII, p. 54 and Nicolini, *Cultura neolatina*, pp. 143-150.
2. *Les fais et bonnes meurs du Sage Roy Charles V*, Vol. I, p. 41.
3. Solente, Introduction, p. iv to *Les fais et bonnes meurs etc.*
4. Although Fantuzzi, *op. cit.*, as early as 1787 made it plain that the name de Pisan (or Pizan) was a French form of Pizzano, the belief that on the contrary Christine came from Pisa persisted among some scholars even as late as 1927. See Pinet, *Christine de Pisan, Etude biographique et littéraire*, p. 3.
5. pp. 49-81.
6. For descriptions of this *hôtel* and quotations from documents concerning it see Bournon, 'L'Hôtel-Royal de Saint-Pol', *Mémoires de la Société de l'Histoire de Paris et de l'Ile de France*, Vol. VI.
7. For these transactions see Solente, Introduction, pp. vii and viii to *Les fais et bonnes meurs*, and Stein 'Christine de Pisan en Gâtinais', in *Annales de la société historique et archéologique du Gâtinais*, Vol XI, pp. 163-165.
8. See, for example, *Oeuvres Poétiques*, Vol. I, pp. 8 and 16.
9. *Les fais et bonnes meurs*, Vol. I, pp. 50-51. Christine referred again to these great processions with the same admiration, in a book which she wrote ten years later, *Le Livre de la Paix*.

CHAPTER TWO

1. *La Mutacion de Fortune*, Vol. I, p. 40.
2. For the *ballades* from which these quotations come see *Oeuvres Poétiques*, Vol. I, pp. 216, 237.
3. For these facts see references given in Chapter One, note 7.

4. In her *Fais et bonnes meurs*, Vol. I, p. 41 Christine definitely says that her mother, 'with her children and myself' were transported to France. But on the few other occasions when she speaks of her brothers the implication always is that they were younger than she.

5. Solente. Introduction, p. x, *op. cit.*

6. *Fais et bonnes meurs*, Vol. I, p. 179.

7. *Lavision*, p. 84.

8. *Fais et bonnes meurs*, Vol. I, p. 170. The remaining quotations and the facts in this and the following paragraphs are all from *Les fais et bonnes meurs*, Vol. I, pp. 16, 153-159 and 161.

9. *The Antient Chronicle of Sir John Froissart*, trans. by John Bourchier, Lord Berners, Vol. IV, pp. 43-46 (1814 ed.).

10. *Oeuvres Poétiques*, Vol. I, pp. 229-230.

11. Berty et Tisserand, *Histoire générale de Paris*, pp. 45-46.

12. This passage occurs in *La Cité des Dames*, a work which has not yet been published. The quotation is taken from the sixteenth-century English translation of it, on which see Chapter Twelve and the Appendix, *Christine and England*.

13. *Le Chemin de Longue Estude*, p. 4.

CHAPTER THREE

1. *Le Chemin de Longue Estude*, p. 6.

2. *Mutacion de Fortune*, pp. 51-53. This is an important passage, for Christine was always very conscious of what, for a good part of her life, seemed to her the baneful influence of the goddess Fortune, a figure generally considered in the Middle Ages to be very powerful. Christine later changed her attitude (see Chapter Eleven below).

3. *Oeuvres Poétiques*, Vol. I, pp. 213-214.

4. *Ibid.*, Vol. I, pp. 1-20.

5. *Ibid.*, Vol. I, pp. 21-100.

6. Solente, Introduction, p. xviii, *op. cit.* and Nicolini *Cultura neolatina*, p. 150, note 46.

7. Nicolini, *op. cit.*, pp. 145-146.

8. *Oeuvres Poétiques*, Vol. III, pp. 27-44.

9. *Ibid.*, Vol. III, pp. 45-57.

10. *Ibid.*, Vol. I., pp. 148-185.

11. *Ibid.*, Vol. I., pp. 207-279.

CHAPTER FOUR

1. *Oeuvres Poétiques*, Vol. II, pp. 1-27.

2. It is possible that Christine did not herself invent some of these arguments. Paul Meyer, 'Mélanges de Poésie Française' in *Romania*, VI, pp. 481-501, mentions a 'Cambridge manuscript' which he says uses some of them, but gives no reference for it. Some of Christine's French predecessors may have thought of them too. But she uses them with such relish as to make them seem her own.

3. See 'Le Livre des faicts du Maréchal Boucicaut' in Michaud et Poujoulat, *Nouvelle Collection des Mémoires*, 1st series, Vol. II, pp. 254-257.

4. For the *ballades* mentioned in this paragraph, see *Oeuvres Poétiques*, Vol. I, pp. 220-221, 224-225, and 208-211.

5. *Le Livre des Fais et Bonnes Meurs*, pp. 26-29.

6. *Lavision*, pp. 165-166.

7. *Oeuvres Poétiques*, Vol. I, pp. 232-233. Louis apparently demanded higher standards among his courtiers than did Henry IV!

8. There is as yet no modern edition of this poem. On the probable date of it, and the identity of 'Hector', see Warner's edition of a contemporary English translation. *The Epistle of Othea to Hector, or The Boke of Knyghthode*, Introduction, pp. xviii, xix, and Campbell, *L'Epitre d'Othea, Etude sur les sources de Christine de Pisan*, pp. 24-30. See also my Appendix, Christine and England, pp. 162–163.

9. On the possible explanation of the name Othea for the goddess of wisdom, see Warner, *op. cit.* Introduction, p. xix and Campbell, *op. cit.*, pp. 31-33.

10. Some of her sources are not far to seek. For her knowledge of the tale of Troy, one of the main ancient legends beloved of the Middle Ages, she might have chosen any one of the versions current from the twelfth century onwards, of which the most popular was *La vraye ystoire de Troye*. Her references to Greek gods and goddesses she almost certainly derived from Ovid, probably from a French version called *Ovid Moralisé*, which was widely read. There were anthologies of quotations from the Fathers, the Bible and the ancient philosophers. On this question see Warner, *op. cit.* Introduction, pp. xxi-xxiv and Campbell, *op. cit., passim*.

11. It was printed under the title *Les Cent histoires de troye* by Philippe Pigouchet, in a beautiful quarto undated, but of the fifteenth century. The subtitle given is *Lepistre de Othea la deesse de prudence envoyee a lesperit chevalereux Hector de Troye, avec cent histoires*; but there is no mention of his being fifteen and, more curious still, no mention of Christine. Yet her dedication to Louis of Orleans is given on the reverse of the title page.

12. *Cambell, op. cit.*, pp. 9-16.

13. This is MS. 9392 in the Bibliothèque Royale, Brussels, which was made for Philip the Good, Duke of Burgundy. It is a wonderfully rich MS, both for the variety of the costumes in which the unknown artist portrays all the characters, both male and female, and the architecture, from palaces to village houses.

CHAPTER FIVE

1. *Oeuvres Poétiques*, Vol. II, pp. 159-222.

2. *Ibid.*, Vol. II, pp. 111-157.

3. *Ibid.*, Vol. II, pp. 49-109.

4. On Louis' many houses see Sauval, *Histoire et recherche des antiquités de la ville de Paris*, Vol. II, p. 115 *et. seq.*

5. *Oeuvres Poétiques*, Vol. I, pp. 231-232.

CHAPTER SIX

1. *Oeuvres Poétiques*, Vol. III, pp. 59-208.

2. For the *ballades* mentioned in this paragraph see *Oeuvres Poétiques*, Vol. I, pp. 277-279. The only mystery about these poems is that Christine calls the young man Duke of Bourbon, whereas he was then still only the Count of Clermont and did not succeed his father until ten years later, i.e. in 1410. This mystery appears insoluble.

3. Ward, *The Epistles on the Romance of the Rose and other documents in the debate*.

4. *Oeuvres Poétiques*, Vol. I, pp. 250-251.

5. *Ibid.*, Vol. I, p. 249.

6. *Ibid.*, Vol. I, pp. 225-226.

7. In the manuscript on which Ward based his edition of the documents in the debate, Christine's letter to the queen is prefaced by a note stating that the letters she is sending are by Gontier Col, Jean the Provost of Lille and Pierre Col, as well as herself. But as the letter from Pierre Col was not written until after Gerson wrote his, in May 1402 (see pp. 69-70), Christine could not have included it in the packet she sent to the queen on February 2nd, 1402. Curiously enough Ward does not mention this fact in his introduction; and Piaget, in his *Chronologie des Epistres sur le Roman de la Rose*, does not refer to the matter, merely stating that in another manuscript (Bibliothèque Nationale MSS, fr. 604) the name of Pierre Col is not mentioned. So the only possible explanation of the note in the manuscript

used by Ward is that it was not by Christine but was added by the later hand of someone who had not checked the contents of the packet.

CHAPTER SEVEN

1. See Piaget, 'La cour amoureuse, dite de Charles VI', *Romania*, Vol. XX, pp. 417-454.
2. She does in fact mention it in her *Mutacion de Fortune*, Vol. I, p. 42.
3. *Oeuvres Poétiques*, Vol. II, pp. 29-48. Roy, editor of the poetry, says it was 'a réunion que l'on pourrait peut-être supposer imaginaire, mais qui à notre avis a dû certainement avoir lieu'.

CHAPTER EIGHT

1. *Oeuvres Poétiques*, Vol. I, p. 98.
2.   'Il n'est si beaulx mestiers,
         Ne qui face gens si entiers'
   It is noteworthy that Charles of Orleans, the poet son of Louis, thirty or forty years later used almost precisely Christine's words when he wrote 'Il n'est nul si beau mestier!' to describe the pleasure that solitary meditation 'playing with his thoughts', gave him. Yet it is not very likely that he ever saw the manuscript in which alone this quotation of Christine's occurs (Harleian 4431) in a poem addressed to the queen, Isabeau of Bavaria, even though this manuscript reached London while he was still a prisoner in England (see page 138).
3. See Delisle, 'Le Cabinet des Manuscripts de la Bibliothèque Impériale' in the *Histoire Générale de Paris*, Vol. 7. See also Boivin le Cadet, *Bibliothèque du Louvre sous les rois Charles V, VI et VII*, a short *dissertation historique*, prefacing the 1836 edition of Gilles Malet's *Inventaire du catalogue des livres de l'ancienne Bibliothèque du Louvre fait en l'année 1373*. See also the catalogue of the exhibition, *La Librarie de Charles V*, at the Bibliothèque Nationale, Paris 1968.
4. See Campbell, Etude sur les sources de Christine de Pisan, in his *L'Epitre d'Othea*, pp. 37-44. But more especially see Solente, *Le Livre de la Mutacion de Fortune*, Vol. I, where her Introduction, pp. xxxiv-xcviii, contains a notable, detailed study of Christine's sources, quoting long passages for comparative purposes.
5. *Oeuvres Poétiques*, Vol. I, pp. 44-45.

CHAPTER NINE

1. 'Englaische pour le temps.' Orthography in Christine's day was still unsettled, but the anglicised spelling she has chosen for 'anglais' seems to

add to the impression that the French did indeed consider that territory as English. See *Le Livre des fais et bonnes meurs*, Vol. I, p. 125.

2. Juvenal des Ursins, *Histoire de Charles VI*, pp. 421-422.

3. *Oeuvres Poétiques*, Vol. I, pp. 240-244.

4. *Chronique*, Vol. I, pp. 39-43.

5. *Oeuvres Poétiques*, Vol. I, pp. 245-246.

6. The quotations in this account, especially of the names of the weapons mentioned in the footnote, are taken from the English translation of Monstrelet's chronicle by Thomas Johnes, Vol. I, p. 16-18.

7. *Oeuvres Poétiques*, Vol. II, pp. 223-294.

8. *Ibid.*, See Roy's note, Vol. II, pp. xvii-xx.

9. *Ibid.*, Vol. III, pp. 1-26.

10. *Ibid.*, Vol. I, p. 251.

11. *Le Chemin de Longue Estude* was one of the only four books by Christine to be published in the century after her death; the others had to wait until the nineteenth century, while some still await publication. But the book that was brought out by Jan Chaperon in 1549, although he states that it was by 'Dame Christine de Pise', is only a very free rendering of her text, full of extraneous matter, which he says was originally written in 'langue Romanne' (whatever that may mean), and which he himself has translated into French. Another curious fact is that he dedicates the book to a woman, Damoyselle Nicole Bataille, hoping that this book by another woman will convince her that the ill report she has had of him is a blasphemy.

CHAPTER TEN

1. Christine opens her history of Charles V with this vivid little account of how it was commissioned.

2. For a fuller study of Christine's sources, from which this account is taken, see Solente's Introduction, pp. xlii-lxxix, to her edition of *Les fais et bonnes meurs*.

3. *Oeuvres Poétiques*, Vol. I, pp. 255-257.

4. *Ordonnances des roys de France*, Vol. XI, pp. 26-32.

5. Luce, in *La France pendant la guerre de cent ans aux xive et xve siècles* 2e série 1893, pp. 46-65 translates the *Relation Latine* 'à peu près littéralement en français'. He says the text was discovered 'il y a quelques années' by M. Hauréau and quotes *Notices et extraits des manuscrits*, t. xxxi, 2e partie, pp. 4-10. Luce also gives a list of the king's closest councillors and

officials who might have written this text, and surmises that the likeliest was Philippe de Mézières.

6. See his 'Notices de deux ouvrages manuscrits de Christine de Pisan' published by Mlle de Keralio, *Collection des meilleurs ouvrages françois composés par des femmes*, Vol. II, pp. 128-129.

CHAPTER ELEVEN

1. *Oeuvres Poétiques*, Vol. II, pp. 295-301.

2. Deschamps, *Oeuvres Complètes*, Vol. IV, p. 169.

3. *Ibid.*, Vol. VI, pp. 26-32.

4. This idea was first put forward by Robineau, *Christine de Pisan*, pp. 224-225. This work, one of the earliest on the subject of Christine (1882), is also one of the best.

5. Juvenal des Ursins, *Histoire de Charles VI*, pp. 431-433; Monstrelet, *Chronique*, Vol. I, pp. 108-125; Nicolas de Baye, *Le Journal*, pp. 137-139.

6. Juvenal des Ursins, *op. cit.*, p. 433.

7. This letter is quoted in full by Thomassy, *Essai sur les écrits politiques de Christine de Pisan*, pp. 133-140.

CHAPTER TWELVE

1. Thomassy, *op. cit.*, p. 128, quotes an extract from the *Chambre des Comptes*, which vividly records these facts: A demoiselle Christine de Pisan, veuve d'Etienne de Castel, cent escus en récompense de deux livres présentés par elle a monseigneur le duc de Bourgogne, dont l'un fut commandé par feu monseigneur de duc de Bourgogne, et l'autre, monseigneur l'a voulu; lesquels livres et autres de ses écrits et dittiez mondit seigneur a trés agréables, et aussi pour compassion et en aumosnes pour employer en mariage d'une sienne povre niece qu'elle a mariee. Par mandement dudit seigneur duc à Paris, le 20 fevrier 1405 [new dating 1406].

2. Solente quotes it in her edition of *Les fais et bonnes meurs*, Vol. II, Appendices 15 and 16, pp. 206-208.

3. Solente, 'Christine de Pisan', in *l'Histoire littéraire de la France*, Vol. XL, pp. 57-59. The MS is B.N. f. fr. No. 5037, ff. 182-221.

4. Champion, *La Librairie de Charles d'Orléans*, p. lxxii.

5. Laborde, *Les Ducs de Bourgogne*, Vol. III, No. 6631 and McLeod, *Charles of Orleans*, Appendix III, p. 356.

6. As Solente says it is, *Ibid.*, p. 59, note 2. She does not mention the description of it quoted in the 1442 inventory.

7. See her *Livre de la Paix*, p. 174.

8. On Anastaise, see Martin, *La Miniature française du xiii au xvi siècles*, pp. 72-75.

CHAPTER THIRTEEN

1. See Solente, 'Christine de Pisan', in *l'Histoire littéraire de la France*, Vol. XL, p. 47.

2. See Le Glay, *Correspondence de l'Empereur Maximilien I et de Marguerite d'Autriche de 1507-1519*, Vol. II, p. 485.

3. There is still no modern critical edition of the *Trésor*, for that promised by Mathilde Laigle, in her *Le Livre des Trois Vertus . . . son milieu historique et littéraire*, has never appeared. She does, however, in this volume quote large extracts from it and it is from these that the translations given in the following pages are taken.

4. These early editions, by Antoine Verard, Michel Lenoir and Jehan et Denis Janot are extremely rare.

5. In *Lavision*, written in 1405, she had said that by then she had written fifteen principal volumes, not counting 'sundry little ditties'. As it was after that date that she wrote the *Lettre à la reine Isabeau*, the *Prodomye de l'Homme*, the *Corps de Policie*, the *Cité des Dames* and the *Trésor*, this would make twenty works in all, though we cannot of course be sure that she would have counted her letter to the queen as a principal work, or included the *Prodomye de l'Homme*, which was more of a translation than an original work.

6. Harleian 4431. Roy, *Oeuvres Poétiques*, Vol. III, pp. xxi-xxiv, quotes a note by Paul Meyer, who says that according to the signatures on the fly-leaf of Vol. I of the MS (which is in two volumes) it was probably acquired by the Duke of Bedford from the collection of Charles VI in 1425 (after the king's death). He gave it to Jacquette de Luxembourg whom he married in 1432 and her name is on it, as well as those of all the subsequent owners down to the Earl of Oxford, in whose keeping it remained until his Harleian collection was bought by Act of Parliament in 1753. It was Sir Frederick Madden, keeper of the manuscripts in the British Museum, who first revealed, from the signatures on the fly-leaf, the owners to whom the manuscript had belonged before it was acquired by the British Museum.

7. For this supposition see Martin, *La Miniature française du xiii-xvi siècles*, p. 75.

8. *Oeuvres Poétiques*, Vol. III, pp. 209-317. On these poems see Roy, Vol. III, Introduction, pp. xvi-xix.

9. *Ibid.*, Vol. I, Introduction, pp. xiv-xvii.

10. *Ibid.*, Vol. I, Introduction, p. ix.

11. Thomassy, *op. cit.*, p. xlvii, footnote.

12. *Op. cit.*, p. 85.

13. Thomassy, *op. cit.*, quotes this poem, pp. 99-101.

14. Solente, in *l'Histoire littéraire etc.*, pp. 66-68.

15. The printed version by Anthoine Vérard appeared in 1488; another by Philippe le Noir came out in 1527 but is only a poor copy of Vérard's edition.

CHAPTER FOURTEEN

1. Roy, *Oeuvres Poétiques*, Vol. I, Introduction, p. x.

2. See Delisle, *Notice sur les Sept Psaumes allegorisés de Christine de Pisan.*

3. Quoted in full by Thomassy, *op. cit.*, pp. 141-149.

4. No manuscripts of this work exist.

5. The manuscript of this work (Bib. Nat. f. fr. 24786, ff. 36-47) was discovered by Solente, who published an account of it with extracts under the title 'Un traité inédit de Christine de Pisan, L'Epistre de la prison de vie humaine' in the *Bibliothèque des Chartes, Vol. LXXXV*, 1924, pp. 263-301. She says (p. 267) that former writers on Christine de Pisan had thought there were no works of hers between 1414 and 1429, but she has found two.

6. This consists of a Latin sentence 'Notandum est quod Christine fuit domina praeclara natu et moribus et manebit in domo religiosarum apud Passye prope Paris'. This sentence was inserted by William Worcester, secretary to Sir John Fastolf (on whom see the Appendix, Christine and England, page 162), who lived in Paris during the English domination, in a manuscript of *The Boke of Noblesse*, a text addressed to King Edward the Fourth in 1475, which exists in a single copy in the British Museum (Royal MS 18B, xxii). See Warner, *The Epistle of Othea to Hector*, Introduction, p. xliii and *Lavision*, p. 9.

7. This is the other manuscript discovered by Mlle Solente. See her 'Un traité inédit'; pp. 267-268 where she quotes the opening paragraph of the manuscript (Bib. Nat. MSS nouv. acq. fr. 10059, ff. 114-145).

8. Quoted in full in Thomassy, *op. cit.*, Introduction, pp. xlii-xlvii.

APPENDIX

1. On all this see Warner, *The Epistle of Othea to Hector, or the Boke of Knyghthode*, Introduction, pp. xxv-xxxvi.

2. See Campbell, *L'Epitre d'Othea, Etude sur les sources* etc., pp. 48-49.

3. Rivers' translation was reprinted from Caxton's edition in 1859 in a limited edition of 95 copies for presentation by William Blades with introductory remarks. On it see also Roy, *op. cit.*, Vol. III, Introduction, p. viii.

4. A note in a modern hand on the fly-leaf of this manuscript says that it was John Talbot, Earl of Shrewsbury, who gave her the book on this occasion; but it was the Earl of Suffolk, not Shrewsbury, who went on this mission.

5. Caxton's translation and edition was reprinted and published for the Early English Text Society in 1932, edited by A. T. P. Byles. For the information in this paragraph see pp. xxix-xxx of his introduction and p. 291 of the text.

Bibliography

THE WORKS OF CHRISTINE DE PIZAN

The works listed below will be found with their full titles in the main bibliography under the names of their editors, commentators, or occasionally translators, as the case may be, given here in brackets after their titles.

POETICAL WORKS

Ballades, rondeaux, oroysons, etc. (Roy)
Enseignemens moraux (Roy and Blades)
Proverbes moraux (Roy and Blades)
Epistre au Dieu d'Amours (Roy)
L'Epistre d'Othéa à Hector (Warner, Campbell and Pigouchet)
Le Livre des Dit de Poissy (Roy)
Le Livre des Trois Jugemens (Roy)
Le Débat de Deux Amants (Roy)
Le Duc des Vrais Amants
Cent ballades d'Amant et de Dame (Roy)
Le Dit de la Rose (Roy)
Le Dit de la Pastoure (Roy)
Three religious poems (Roy)
Le Livre de la Mutacion de Fortune (Solente)
The Letter to Eustache Morel (Roy)

PROSE WORKS

The letters in the debate on the *Roman de la Rose* (Ward)
Le Chemin de longue estude (Pueschel)
Le livre des fais et bonnes meurs de Charles V (Solente)
Lavision (Towner)
The Letter to Queen Isabeau (Thomassy)
La Prod'homie de l'homme (unpublished)
Le Livre du Corps de Policie (Lucas)
La Cité des Dames (unpublished, but see Anslay)
Le Trésor de la Cité des Dames (unpublished)
Sept Psaumes allegorisés (Delisle and Raine)

178

BIBLIOGRAPHY

Lamentation sur les maux de la guerre civile (Thomassy)
Le Livre des fais d'armes et de chevalerie (unpublished, but see Byles)
Le Livre de la paix (Willard)
L'epistre de la prison de vie humaine (Solente)
Les heures de contemplation de Nostre Seigneur (Solente)
Hymn to Joan of Arc (Thomassy)

Anslay, Bryan (tr.), *The Cyte of Ladyes*, London, 1521.

Barrois, J., *Bibliothèque Protypographique*, Paris, 1810.

Baye, Nicolas de, Greffier du Parlement de Paris, 1400-1417, *Le Journal*, ed. A. Tuetey, for the Société de l'Histoire de France, 2 vol., Paris, 1885.

Berty, A. and Tisserand, L.-M., *Topographic historique de vieux Paris*, 6 vols., Paris, 1866-97.

Blades, W. (ed.), *Morale Proverbes, composed in French by Cristyne de Pisan, translated by the Earl Rivers,* reprinted from the original edition of William Caxton, A.D. 1478, with introductory remarks by William Blades, London, 1859.

Boivin le cadet, 'Vie de Christine de Pisan', in Keralio, Mlle de, *Collection des meilleurs ouvrages françois* etc., Vol. II, Paris, 1787.

'Bibliothèque du Louvre sous les rois Charles V, Charles VI, et Charles VII, dissertation historique prefacing Gilles Malet's *Inventaire du Catalogue des livres dè l'ancienne bibliothèque du Louvre* . . . 1373, reprinted Paris, 1836.

Boriès, E., *Histoire de la ville de Poissy*, Paris, 1901.

Boucicaut, Maréchal, *Le Livre des faicts du*, in Michaud et Poujoulat, *Nouvelle Collection des mémoires pour servir à l'histoire de France*, Série I, Vol. II, Paris, 1836.

Bournon, F., L'Hôtel Royal de Saint Pol, *Mémoires de la Société de l'Histoire de Paris et de l'Ile-de-France*, Vol. VI, Paris, 1879.

Byles, A. T. P. (ed.), *The Book of fayttes of armes and of chyvalry, translated and printed by William Caxton from the French of Christine de Pisan,* ed. A. T. P. Byles for the Early English Text Society, O.U.P., 1937.

Campbell, F.-G.-C., *L'Epitre d'Othéa, Etude sur les sources de Christine de Pisan,* Paris, 1924.

Castel, Mme Etienne du, *Ma grand-mère Christine de Pisan*, Paris, 1936.

Castel, Françoise du, *Damoiselle Christine de Pisan*, Paris, 1973.

Champion, Pierre, *Histoire poétique du XVe siècle*, 2 vol., Paris, 1923.
Splendeurs et misères de Paris, XIV-XVe siècles, Paris, 1934.
La Librairie de Charles d'Orléans, Paris, 1910.

Delisle, L. V., *Le Cabinet des manuscrits de la Bibliothèque Impériale*, 3 vol., Paris, 1868-1881.
Notice sur les Sept Psaumes allégorisés de Christine de Pisan, Paris 1896.
Recherches sur la librairie de Charles V, Paris, 1907.

Deschamps, Eustache, *Oeuvres complètes*, ed. by Le Marquis de Queux de Saint-Hilaire et M. G. Raynaud, 10 vol., Paris, 1878-1903.

Fantuzzi, G., *Notizie degli scrittori bolognesi*, Vol. VII, Bologna, 1781-1784.

Favier, M., *Christine de Pisan, muse des cours souveraines*, Lausanne, 1967.

Felibien, D. M. A., *Histoire de la ville de Paris*, Paris, 1725.

Froissart, J., *The Antient Chronicles of Sir John Froissart, translated from the original French by . . . Lord Berners*, 4 vol., reprinted London, 1814.

Jorga, N., *Philippe de Mézières*, 1327-1405, Paris, 1896.

Juvenal des Ursins, Jean, *Histoire de Charles VI, Roy de France*, etc. in Michaud et Poujoulat, *Nouvelle Collection des mémoires pour servir à l'histoire de France*, Série 1, Vol. II, Paris, 1836.

Kemp-Welch, A., *Of Six Mediaeval Women*, London, 1913.
The Book of the Duke of True Lovers, trans. with an introduction by A. Kemp-Welch, the ballads rendered into the original metres by Laurence Binyon and Eric Maclagan, London, 1908.

Keralio, Mlle de, *Collection des meilleurs ouvrages françois, composés par des femmes*, Vol. II and III, Paris, 1787.

Laborde, L. de (Conte), *Les Ducs de Bourgogne*, 3 vol., Paris, 1849-52.

Laigle, M., *Le Livre des Trois Vertus de Christine de Pisan et son milieu historique et littéraire*, Paris, 1912.

Lavisse, E., *Histoire de France*, Vol. IV, Paris, 1901.

Lebeuf, J., *Histoire de la ville de Paris*, ed. H. Cocheris, Paris, 1863-67.

Le-Franc, Martin, *Le Champion des Dames*, 1530, reprinted Paris, 1874.

Le Gentil, P., *Christine de Pisan, poète méconnu*, Paris, 1951.

Le Glay, A. J. G., *Correspondence de l'Empereur Maximilien I et Marguerite d'Autriche*, 1507-1519, Vol. II, Paris, 1839.

Lucas, R. H. (ed.), *Christine de Pisan, Le Livre du Corps de Policie*, Geneva and Paris, 1967.

Luce, S., *La France pendant la guerre de Cent Ans*, Paris, 1893.

Martin, H. M. R., *La Miniature française du XIIIe au XVe siècles*, Paris et Bruxelles, 1923.

Meiss, Millard, *French painting in the time of Jean de Berry*, London, 1967.

Metz, Guillaume de, *Description de la ville de Paris au XVe siècle*, ed. Leroux de Lincy, Paris, 1855.

Meung, Jean de, *Le Roman de la Rose, mis en français moderne*, Paris, 1949.

BIBLIOGRAPHY

Meyer, Paul, 'Mélanges de poésie française' in *Romania*, Vol. VI, Paris, 1877.

Monstrelet, Enguerrand de, *La Chronique*, ed. L. Douët d'Arcq, for the Société de l'histoire de France, 6 vol., Paris, 1857-62.

Monstrelet, E. de, *The Chronicles*, trans. by Thomas Johnes. 2 vol., London, 1840.

Nicolini, E., 'Cristine da Pizzano, l'origine e il nome' in *Bollettino dell' Istituto di filologia romanza della R. Università di Romà*, Anno I, fasc. II, Modena, 1941.

Noël, O., *Histoire de la ville de Poissy depuis ses origines jusqu'à nos jours*, Poissy, 1869.

Nys, E., *Christine de Pisan et ses principales oeuvres*, Bruxelles, 1914.
Honoré Bonet et Christine de Pisan, Bruxelles, 1882.

Piaget, A., 'Chronologie des Epistres sur le Roman de la Rose', in *Etudes romanes dédiées à Gaston Paris*, Paris, 1891.
'La cour amoureuse dite de Charles VI,' in *Romania*, Vol. XX, Paris, 1891.

Picard, A., 'Bureau de la Rivière, favori de Charles V et de Charles VI'. *Ecole des Chartes, Positions de Thèses*, Paris, 1889.

Pigouchet, P., *Les cent histoires de troyes*, Paris, 1490.

Pinet, M.-J., *Christine de Pisan, 1364-1430, Etude biographique et littéraire*, Paris, 1927.

Pueschel, R., *Le Chemin de long estude, par Christine de Pizan*, Berlin, 1881.

Raine, R. R., *Les Sept Psaumes allégorises de Christine de Pisan, a critical edition*, Washington, 1965.

Rigaud, R., *Les idées féministes de Christine de Pisan*, Neuchâtel, 1911.

Robineau, E. M.-D., *Christine de Pisan, sa vie, ses oeuvres*, Saint-Omer, 1882.

Roy, M., *Oeuvres poétiques de Christine de Pisan*, ed. for the Société des anciens textes français, 3 vol., Paris, 1886.

Sauval, H. *Histoire et recherche des antiquités de Paris*, Paris, 1724.

Solente, S. (ed.), *Le Livre de la Mutacion de Fortune, par Christine de Pisan*, publ. S. Solente for the Société des Anciens textes français, 4 vol., Paris, 1959-68.
Le Livre des fais et bonnes meurs du sage roy Charles V, par Christine de Pisan, publ. pour le Société de l'Histoire de France par S. Solente, 2 vol., Paris, 1936.
'A propos d'un livre récent sur Christine de Pisan', in *Revue belge de philologie et d'histoire*, Vol. VIII, Brussels, 1929.
'Un traité inédit de Christine de Pisan, l'Epistre de la prison de vie humaine,' (there are some notes on the *Heures de Contemplation de Nostre Seigneur* with this too) in *Bibliothèque de l'Ecole des Chartes, Vol. LXXXV*, Paris, 1924.

'Christine de Pisan', in *l'Histoire littéraire de la France*, Vol. XL, Paris, 1869.

Stein, H., 'Christine de Pisan en Gâtinais', in *Annales de la société historique et archéologique du Gâtinais*, Vol. XI, Fontainebleu, 1893.

Thomassy, R., *Essai sur les écrits politiques de Christine de Pisan, Suivi d'une notice littéraire et de pièces inédits*, (among which are the *Lettre à la reine Isabelle*, the *Lamentation sur les maux de la guerre civile*, and the *Hymn to Jeanne d'Arc*).

Towner, M. L., *Lavision-Christine*, introduction and text, Washington, 1932.

Ward, C. F. (ed.), *The Epistles on the Romance of the Rose and other documents in the debate, with a dissertation*, University of Chicago, 1911.

Warner, G. F., *The Epistle of Othea to Hector, or the Boke of Knyghthode*, translated from the French of Christine de Pisan . . . by Stephen Scrope, edited from a manuscript in the library of the Marquis of Bath by George F. Warner, London, 1904.

Willard, C. C., *The Livre de la Paix of Christine de Pisan*, a critical edition with introduction and notes, 's Gravenhage, 1958.

Index

Page references are only given for the most significant matters or events in the lives of the main characters mentioned. Men are listed under their titles or surnames, women under their Christian names. Names mentioned in the appendix are not listed.

INDEX

INDEX